D0457276

GREAT TALES
FROM
ENGLISH HISTORY

Also by Robert Lacey

ROBERT, EARL OF ESSEX

THE LIFE AND TIMES OF HENRY VIII

THE QUEENS OF THE NORTH ATLANTIC

SIR WALTER RALEGH

MAJESTY: ELIZABETH II AND THE HOUSE OF WINDSOR

THE KINGDOM

PRINCESS

ARISTOCRATS

FORD: THE MEN AND THE MACHINE

GOD BLESS HER!

QUEEN MOTHER

LITTLE MAN

GRACE

SOTHEBY'S: BIDDING FOR CLASS

THE YEAR 1000

THE QUEEN MOTHER'S CENTURY

ROYAL: HER MAJESTY QUEEN ELIZABETH II

GREAT TALES
FROM
ENGLISH
HISTORY

*The Truth about King Arthur,
Lady Godiva, Richard the Lionheart
and More*

ROBERT LACEY

 LITTLE, BROWN AND COMPANY
New York ✢ Boston

Little, Brown and Company
Time Warner Book Group
1271 Avenue of the Americas, New York, NY 10020
Visit our Web site at www.twbookmark.com

First published in Great Britain by Little, Brown, 2003
First United States edition, 2004

The author gratefully acknowledges permission to quote from
Bede: Ecclesiastical History of the English People (Penguin Classics, 1995;
revised edition, 1968), translation copyright © Leo Sherley-Price, 1955, 1968;
The Ecclesiastical History of Orderic Vitalis (Oxford, Clarendon Press, 1978),
translator Marjorie Chibnall, © Oxford University Press, 1978;
The Anglo-Saxon Chronicle (J. M. Dent, 1996),
translator M. J. Swanton, © J. M. Dent, 1996;
Piers the Ploughman by William Langland (Penguin Books, 1966),
translation © J. F. Goodridge, 1959, 1966.

Illustrations and maps © 2003 by Fred van Deelen

ISBN 0-316-10910-X
LCCN 2003115660

10 9 8 7 6 5 4 3 2 1

Q–MB

Printed in the United States of America

FOR SASHA

CONTENTS

CONTENTS

Anglo-Saxon and Norman England

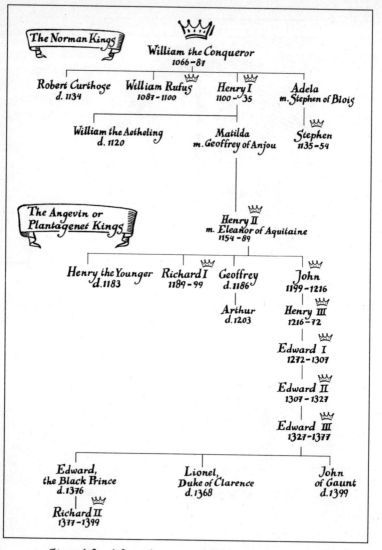

The Norman Kings

William the Conqueror
1066-87

Robert Curthose
d. 1134

William Rufus
1087-1100

Henry I
1100-35

Adela
m. Stephen of Blois

William the Aetheling
d. 1120

Matilda
m. Geoffrey of Anjou

Stephen
1135-54

The Angevin or
Plantagenet Kings

Henry II
m. Eleanor of Aquitaine
1154-89

Henry the Younger
d. 1183

Richard I
1189-99

Geoffrey
d. 1186

John
1199-1216

Arthur
d. 1203

Henry III
1216-72

Edward I
1272-1307

Edward II
1307-1327

Edward III
1327-1377

Edward,
the Black Prince
d. 1376

Lionel,
Duke of Clarence
d. 1368

John
of Gaunt
d. 1399

Richard II
1377-1399

Simplified family tree of England's Norman and Angevin Kings

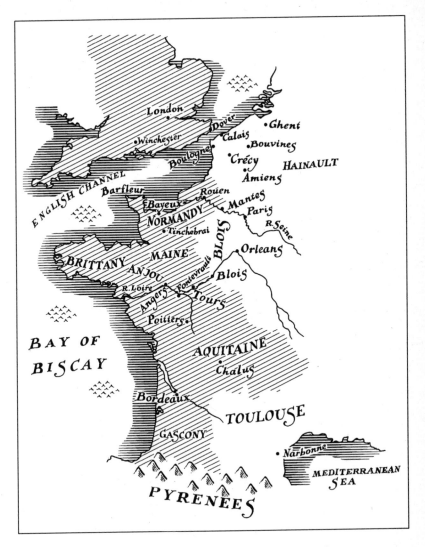

France and Normandy, showing the
Angevin possessions of King Henry II
(Henry Plantagenet) around 1174

STORYTELLING

THE FIRST HISTORY BOOK THAT I REMEMBER reading with pleasure was a stout, blue, exuberantly triumphalist volume, *Our Island Story – A History of England for Boys and Girls* by H. E. Marshall. It had a red and gold crested shield embossed on the cover, and it told tales of men, women and often children whom it dared to describe as 'heroes' and 'heroines'. It was accompanied by a companion volume, *Our Empire Story*, which was still more politically incorrect, relating the sagas of the heroes and heroines who adventured 'across the seas' to paint much of the globe pink. I must confess that I loved it still more – even though I discovered, at the beginning of the second chapter, that the author had a vivid imagination.

John Cabot's ship the *Matthew* was described by Marshall as sailing out from Bristol harbour one bright May morning in 1497, 'followed by the wishes and prayers of many an anxious heart . . . until it was but a speck in the distance'. Old H. E. – who, I later learned, was an Edwardian lady, Henrietta Elizabeth, living and writing in Australia – was clearly not aware that the port of Bristol is several muddy miles inland from the Bristol Channel. As a pupil at Clifton National Infants School, a few hundred yards from the Bristol docks, I could have told her that if there had been a crowd waving goodbye to Cabot in 1497, they would have lost sight of the doughty mariner as he tacked round the first corner of the Avon Gorge.

It was my first lesson in the imperfections of history. There may be such a thing as pure, true history – what actually, really, *definitely* happened in the past – but it is unknowable. We can only hope to get somewhere close. The history that we have to make do with is the story that historians choose to tell us, pieced together and handed down, filtered through every handler's value system and particular axe that he or she chooses to grind.

In fact, I was never that disillusioned by H. E. Marshall's mistake. I was in thrall to the tales that she told – and in our postmodern age it could even be considered healthy to have realised that I was reading not the truth, but someone else's imperfect version of it. 'History' and 'story' derive from the same linguistic root, and if history can never escape its authorship, it should at least try to make the authorship readable and bright.

Unlike English, maths, and science, history is not in the core curriculum of British schools. You can give it up at fourteen, and the minority of pupils (around 5 per cent) who do choose to study history at GCSE and A level are not taken through every reign and century of their country's development. They are offered an episodic menu of currently fashionable topics that are considered 'relevant' – Nazi Germany and Soviet Russia feature prominently under this heading. In fact, the apparently obscure subject of English medieval history would present students with material of much more relevance – the growth and principles of our freedoms, law and Parliamentary system, not to mention the buildings, towns, and countryside that help define our sense of who we are. It would also introduce them to some extraordinary personalities.

Heroes and heroines are judged to have had their day. The un-teaching of history concentrates on 'themes' rather than personalities. But personality – human nature – is surely the essence of history, and I have deliberately made personalities the essence of this book. Brief though each chapter is, *Great Tales* seeks to create a coherent, chronological picture of our island story, while following the guiding principle that all men and women have heroism inside them – along with generous and fascinating measures of incompetence, apathy, evil and lust. This volume makes a start on the history of England. Later will follow the great tales of Ireland, Scotland, and Wales – which may, or may not, add up to an overall anthology of Great Britishness. There are more and richer dimensions to life than nationality, but our sense of community does rest inescapably upon the stories that we recall from our past.

Making due allowance for the Avon Gorge factor, all the tales in these pages are true. I have consulted the best available contemporary sources and eyewitness accounts, and I record my thanks in the acknowledgements to the many historians on whose modern research I have drawn. But telling stories that are 'true' does not exclude England's legends – the romances of King Arthur, Hereward the Wake, or Robin Hood. You will find them examined here as myths that

illustrate a truth about the age from which they spring –
while also revealing how we today like our Englishness to be.

This book seeks to illuminate, but also to entertain, and
looking back at *Our Island Story*, I find that H. E. Marshall
was similarly inspired. In her foreword, she asked her young
readers not to be too cross with her when they grew up, read
'serious' history and discovered the difference between her
beguiling narrative and the less riveting messiness of reality.

'Remember,' she wrote, 'I was not trying to teach you, but
only to tell a story.'

GREAT TALES
FROM
ENGLISH
HISTORY

CHEDDAR MAN

c.7150 BC

THERE WAS A TIME, AS RECENTLY AS NINE thousand years ago, when the British Isles were not islands at all. After the bleakness of the successive ice ages, the south-eastern corner of modern England was still linked to Europe by a wide swathe of low-lying marshes. People crossed to and fro, and so did animals – including antelopes and brown bears. We know this because the remains of these creatures were discovered by modern archaeologists in a cave in the Cheddar Gorge near Bristol. Scattered among numerous wild horse bones, the scraps of bear and antelope had made up the larder of 'Cheddar Man', England's oldest complete skeleton, found lying nearby in the cave with his legs curled up under him.

According to the radiocarbon dating of his bones, Cheddar Man lived and died around 7150 BC. He was a member of one of the small bands of hunter-gatherers who were then padding their way over the soft forest floors of north-western Europe. The dry cave was his home base, where mothers and grandmothers reared children, kindling fires for warmth and lighting and for cooking the family dinner. We don't know what language Cheddar Man spoke. But we can deduce that wild horsemeat was his staple food and that he hunted his prey across the grey-green Mendip Hills with traps, clubs and spears tipped with delicately sharpened leaf-shaped flints.

Did Cheddar Man have a name of his own? A wife or children? Did he have a god to whom he prayed? The answers to all these basic questions remain mysteries. Bone experts tell us that he was twenty-three or so when he died – almost certainly from a violent blow to his head. So our earliest semi-identifiable ancestor could have been a battle casualty, or even a murder victim. And since the pattern of cuts on his bones is the same as the butcher's cuts made on the animal bones around him, we are confronted with another, still more gruesome possibility – that our early ancestors were cannibals. According to some archaeologists, the reason why so few human skeletons survive from these post-ice-age years is because relatives must have eaten the dead, cracking up the bones to suck out the nourishing marrow inside.

As we set out to explore the past, we should keep in mind the first rule of history: the things that we don't know far outnumber the things that we do. And when we do unravel secrets, the results seldom fit in with our own modern opinions of how life should be.

PYTHEAS AND THE
PAINTED PEOPLE

c.325 BC

CHEDDAR MAN HAD LIVED IN AN ERA OF global warming. As the glaciers of the last ice age melted, sea levels were rising sharply, and this turned high ground like the Isle of Wight, the Isle of Man, and modern Ireland into separate islands. The waters flooded over the land bridge, severing the physical link with Europe.

Thus was created the great moat that we now call the English Channel. As you approached England by boat across the narrowest point where marshes had once been, you were confronted by the striking prospect of long, tall cliffs of bright chalk – the inspiration, according to one theory, for the country's earliest recorded name, Albion, from the Celtic word for 'white'. Europe's great white-capped mountain chain, the Alps, are thought to have derived their name from the same linguistic root.

It was Pytheas, a brave and enquiring Greek navigator, who probably wrote down the name around 325 BC. Nearly seven thousand years after the death of Cheddar Man, Pytheas travelled north from the Mediterranean to investigate the islands that were by now supplying the tin which, when smelted and alloyed with copper, produced the bronze for the tools and weapons of southern Europe. These offshore 'tin islands' were so remote that they were said to be occupied by one-eyed men and griffins. But unafraid, Pytheas followed the customary trade routes to Cornwall, and set about composing the earliest written description of this land that lay on the edge of the known world.

The Greek explorer seems to have covered large areas of the country on foot. Placing his gnomon, or surveying-stick, into the ground at noon each day, he was able to measure the changing length of its shadow and hence calculate latitude and the distance north he had travelled. He almost certainly sailed around the islands, and was the first to describe the shape of Britain as a wonky triangle. Rival geographers scorned Pytheas. But his findings, which survive today only in fragments through the writings of others, have been confirmed by time – and by modern archaeologists, whose excavations tell us of a population that had advanced spectacularly since the days of Cheddar Man.

The inhabitants of Albion by now spoke Celtic, a lilting, flexible language distantly related to Latin. They shared it with the Gauls across the water in the Low Countries and

France. They still hunted, as Cheddar Man had done. But now their spears and arrows were tipped with bronze or iron, not sharpened flint, and they no longer depended on hunting for survival. They hunted for pleasure and to supplement a diet that was derived from their farms, since they had learned how to tame both plants and animals. By 300 BC surprisingly large areas of the landscape were a patchwork of open fields – the classic English countryside that we recognise today. Iron axes had cut down the forests. Iron hoes and ploughs had scratched and cross-hatched fields whose boundaries were marked, on the uplands, by firm white furrows that, in some cases, still serve as boundaries for farmers in the twenty-first century.

Compared with Cheddar Man the Celts were quite affluent folk, with jewellery, polished metal mirrors and artfully incised pots decorating their homes. Some lived in towns. The remains of their bulky earth-walled settlements can still be seen in southern England, along with the monuments of their mysterious religion – the sinuous, heart-lifting white horses whose prancings they carved into the soft chalk of the Downs.

They were a people who enjoyed their pleasures, to judge from the large quantities of wine jars that have been dug from their household debris. They brewed their own ale and mead, a high-alcohol fermentation of water and honey which they ceremoniously passed from one to another in loving-cups. And while their sips might be small, it was happily noted in the Mediterranean, where the wine jars came from, that this sipping took place 'rather frequently' – as one ancient historian put it.

But there was a darker side. The religious rituals of these Celts were in the hands of the Druids – high priests or witch doctors, according to your point of view. Travellers told tales of human sacrifice in their sacred groves of oak and mistletoe, and modern excavations have confirmed their altars must have reeked of carrion. One recent dig revealed a body that had been partially drowned and had its blood drained from the jugular vein. Death, it seems, was finally administered by the ritual of garrotting – a technique of crushing the windpipe by twisting a knotted rope around the neck.

The Celts were fearsome in battle, stripping down to their coarse woven undershorts and painting themselves with the greeny-blue dye that they extracted from the arrow-shaped leaves of the woad plant. Woad was the war paint of Albion's inhabitants, and it is thought to have inspired a name that has lasted to this day. *Pretani* is the Celtic for painted, or tattooed folk, and Pytheas seems to have transcribed this into Greek as *pretanniké*, meaning 'the land of the painted people'. When later translated into Latin, *pretanniké* yielded first *Pretannia*, then *Britannia*.

Diodorus Siculus, a historian working in Rome in the first century BC, described a less ferocious aspect of these blue-painted warriors. They were, he said, 'especially friendly to strangers' – always happy to do business with the many foreign merchants who now travelled to Pretannia to purchase Cornish tin, wolfhounds and the odd slave. Hide-covered boats carried the tin across to France, where pack-horses and river barges transported it along the trade routes that led southwards through Italy to Rome. By the first century BC Rome had supplanted Greece as the Western centre of learning and military might. The Roman Empire circled the Mediterranean and had reached north into France and Germany. The wealth of the distant tin islands sounded tempting. As the Roman historian Tacitus later put it, the land of these painted people could be *'pretium victoriae'* – 'well worth the conquering'.

THE STANDARD-BEARER OF
THE 10TH

55 BC

SO FAR IN OUR STORY ALL THE DATES HAVE been estimates – much better than guesses, but not really precise. Radiocarbon dating, for example, measures the rate of decay of the radioactive isotope carbon 14, which is found in all living things but which starts to decay at the moment of death at a precisely predictable rate. Using this method, scientists have been able to calculate the age of Cheddar Man to an accuracy of one hundred and fifty years.

But now, in 55 BC, we can for the first time set a British date precisely in months and days. Two centuries after the travel jottings of Pytheas, our history finally collides full tilt with the culture of writing – and what a writer to start with!

Gaius Julius Caesar not only shaped history – he also wrote about it. Reading his vivid account of his invasion of Britain, we can feel ourselves there with him in the early hours of 26 August 55 BC, rocking in the swell in his creaking wooden vessel off the white cliffs of Albion – and contemplating the unwelcome sight at the top of them.

'Armed men,' he wrote, 'could be seen stationed on all the heights, and the nature of the place was such, with the shore edged by sheer cliffs, that javelins and spears could be hurled onto the beach.'

The Roman force had sailed from France the previous night, cruising through the darkness with a fleet of eighty ships bearing two battle-hardened legions – about ten thousand men. Trying to control the western corner of Europe for Rome, Caesar had found his authority challenged by the Celtic peoples of Gaul, and he had a strong suspicion they had been receiving help from their cousins in Britain. He had tried to get to the bottom of it, calling together the merchants who traded with the Britons across the channel, but he had received no straight answers. His solution had been to spend the summer assembling his invasion fleet, and now, here at the top of the cliffs, was the reception committee.

Caesar ordered his ships to sail along the coast for a few miles to where the cliffs gave way to a sloping beach, somewhere near the modern port of Deal. But the Britons kept pace with him along the cliff top on horseback and in chariots, then coming down to mass together menacingly on the beach. The Roman legionaries faced the unappealing prospect of leaping into chest-high water in their heavy armour and battling their way ashore.

'Our troops,' admitted Caesar, 'were shaken, and they failed to show the same dash and enthusiasm as they did in land battles.'

But then the standard-bearer of the 10th legion leapt down into the waves, brandishing high the silver eagle that was the symbol of the favour in which the gods held the regiment. Dressed in a wild-animal pelt, with the snarling head of a lion, bear or wolf fixed to the top of his helmet, the standard-bearer was guardian of the legion's morale. While the eagle remained upright, the legion's honour lived.

'Jump down, men!' cried the standard-bearer, 'unless you want the enemy to get your standard! You will not find me failing in my duty to my country or my leader!'

According to Caesar, the Roman footsoldiers were transformed by the gallantry of the standard-bearer. Crashing down into the water after him, they fought their way up the shingle to regroup and form the disciplined lines of shields, spears and swords that made up the basic Roman battle formation. The Britons withdrew, and Caesar sent home news of a mighty victory. When his report reached Rome, the Senate voted an unprecedented twenty-day holiday of celebration.

But the Roman conqueror then spent less than twenty days in Britain. A storm wrecked many of his ships, so Caesar headed smartly back to France before the weather got any worse. Next summer, in July 54 BC, he tried again, with redesigned landing craft whose shallow keels could be driven through the waves and up on to the beach. With more cavalry than at their first attempt, the Romans were able to secure their beachhead, march inland and cross the River

Thames, fighting off hit-and-run attacks. The Celtic chiefs that Caesar managed to corner offered the conqueror their allegiance. But once again the winter storms threatened, and the Romans had to hurry back to France. This time the Senate did not call a holiday.

Julius Caesar was one of the megastars of Western history. Tall and sharp-featured, with the thinning brushed-forward hairstyle immortalised in countless marble statues, he was a man of extraordinary charisma. A brilliant general, he fought off his rivals to gain control of the entire Roman Empire before being murdered by opponents of his absolute power. Later Roman emperors tried to borrow his glory by calling themselves Caesar, and his memory has been perpetuated into recent times by the German and Russian titles of Kaiser and Czar.

In 45 BC he reformed the Western calendar. Known henceforward as the Julian calendar, this used the device of the leap year to keep the earthly year in pace with the sun. The month of July is named after him, as is the Caesarean method of delivering babies, deriving from the story that his mother died while giving birth to him and that he had to be cut out of her womb. Ever the self-publicist, he is famous for his declaration 'Veni, vidi, vici' – 'I came, I saw, I conquered' – after his victory at Zela in central Turkey in 47 BC, and he conveyed a similar message of triumphant conquest when writing the history of his two brief trips to Britain. Describing events in words had made the historical record more vivid and accurate in many ways – but words clearly provided no guarantee that history would now become more truthful.

AND DID THOSE FEET?
JESUS CHRIST AND THE
LEGENDS OF GLASTONBURY

AD 1–33

And did those feet in ancient time
Walk upon England's mountains green?
And was the Holy Lamb of God
On England's pleasant pastures seen?

SUNG AT RUGBY MATCHES AND PATRIOTIC occasions like the Last Night of the Proms, the hymn 'Jerusalem' has become England's unofficial national anthem. Its uplifting lines conjure up the wild idea that Jesus Christ himself, 'the Holy Lamb of God', set foot in England at some moment during his thirty-three years on earth. If

Pytheas the Greek and Julius Caesar could make it from the Mediterranean, why not the Saviour?

It could not possibly be. If Christ had had the time and means to travel the five thousand miles all the way from Palestine across Europe to England and back again in the course of his brief life, it would certainly have been recorded in the Gospels. And would not Christ himself have referred to the great adventure somewhere in his teaching?

The myth has entered the folk memory sideways, through the fables inspired by Joseph of Arimathea, the rich disciple who provided the tomb for Christ's body after the crucifixion. The Gospels tell us quite a lot about Joseph (not to be confused with Christ's father, Joseph the carpenter). A well respected member of the Sanhedrin, or Supreme Council of the Jews, Joseph had kept secret his dangerous conversion to the message of Jesus. It was only a man of such standing who could have gone to Pontius Pilate, the Roman governor of Judaea, and asked for Christ's dead body.

But over the centuries – and we are talking of more than a dozen centuries – extra exploits were attributed to this substantial and intriguing character. Joseph is said to have been one of the disciples who travelled to northern Europe preaching the gospel. He was credited with founding the first monastery in Britain. Other tales supposed that he had made his wealth in the metals trade, and had been in the habit of visiting the south-west in search of Cornwall's tin and Somerset's high-quality lead. It was even imagined that Joseph was the uncle of the Virgin Mary, and therefore the great-uncle of Christ, and so might have brought the boy along on one of his business trips to the region.

In 1502 came the first mention of a living relic that might lend some substance to these extraordinary tales – a hawthorn bush growing at Glastonbury Abbey in Somerset. Blossoming unusually around Christmastime, in the depths of winter and on Christ's birthday, it was known as the Holy Thorn and was said to have been planted by Joseph of Arimathea himself when he stuck his staff into the ground and it took root. It was further said that Joseph had cut his staff from the same bush as Christ's crown of thorns – and modern botanists have established that the Glastonbury thorn, a pinkish-flowered hawthorn known as *Crataegus monogyna praecox*, is indeed a plant that originated in the Middle East. It blooms in Glastonbury to this day and the first sprig of blossom is ceremonially cut and presented to the Queen, who keeps it on her desk over Christmas.

In 1808, at the height of Britain's bitter wars against Napoleon, the artist and poet William Blake pulled together the elements of the various Jesus and Glastonbury legends to create the poem that we now know as 'Jerusalem'. Blake was a mystic and a radical, then making his living in a grimy engraving workshop in the sooty slums of London, where he dreamed of angels. He abhorred what he memorably described as the 'dark satanic mills' of industrial Britain, and he nursed the vision that a shining new society might be built. Jerusalem in our own day may be a sadly afflicted and tragically unholy place, but to Blake it was something glorious:

> *Bring me my bow of burning gold!*
> *Bring me my arrows of desire!*

Bring me my spear! O clouds, unfold!
Bring me my chariot of fire!

I will not cease from mental fight,
Nor shall my sword sleep in my hand,
Till we have built Jerusalem,
In England's green and pleasant land.

Two centuries later during the horrors of World War I, when the flower of Europe's youth was being slaughtered in the trenches of northern France, the composer Hubert Parry set the visionary words to music. The first time the stirring strains of 'Jerusalem' were heard in public was at a 'Votes for Women' concert in 1916, setting the note of reform and regeneration that the anthem retains to this day.

Let us say it one more time – we can be as sure as the sun rises that Jesus Christ did not set foot in Glastonbury, or anywhere else in England. The legend of Joseph of Arimathea is not history. But over the centuries the story would play its part in inspiring history. In words and music, 'Jerusalem' gives wing to the sense of hope and shared endeavour that a community needs if it is to believe in itself – the vision of a national spirit as clean and pure as England's beautiful green countryside. Things may be good, but let us not get complacent – 'better must come'.

THE EMPEROR CLAUDIUS
TRIUMPHANT

AD 43

A FTER CAESAR'S HASTY DEPARTURE IN 54 BC, it was more than ninety years before the Romans tried to conquer Britain again – and when they eventually landed, they made the most of their triumph. In AD 43 the forty-thousand-strong army pushed resistance aside as it rolled up through Kent to the Thames, where the men were ordered to halt. The emperor Claudius wanted to catch up with them, and he duly arrived in splendour for the advance into modern Colchester, the principal British settlement of the south-east. The Roman victory parade featured a squadron of elephants, whose exotic appearance must have been greeted with amazement as they plodded through the Kent countryside.

Swaying a dozen feet above the ground, the club-footed but canny Claudius proudly claimed Colchester as the capital of Rome's latest province. Straight streets were laid down, with a forum and amphitheatre, and the showpiece was a high, rectangular, white-pillared temple. Roman veterans were given land around the town, in the centre of which rose a statue of the emperor. With firm chin, large nose and slicked-down hair, the statue made Claudius look remarkably like Julius Caesar.

Claudius was considered a rather comical character by his contemporaries, who secretly mocked his physical handicaps. His dragging right foot was probably the result of brain damage at birth – his head and hands shook slightly – and he had a cracked, throaty and scarcely intelligible voice which, according to one of his enemies, belonged 'to no land animal'. But as someone who had often found himself in the hands of doctors, he had a high regard for healing. He managed a soothing tone when dealing with the local chieftains of Britain, acknowledging that they had rights. He honoured them as 'kings' – which, in turn, boosted his own status as their emperor. Then in AD 54 Claudius died, to be succeeded by his stepson Nero, whose name would become proverbial for wilfulness and cruelty.

BOADICEA, WARRIOR QUEEN

AD 61

ANY BRITISH 'KING' WHO LIVED UNDER THE Romans had to pay a price for his protection. So when Prasutagus, the leader of the Iceni people, died in AD 60 he prudently left half his wealth and territories to the emperor Nero as a form of 'death duty'. The Iceni occupied the flat fenlands that stretched down from the Wash across modern Norfolk and Suffolk and, like other Celtic peoples, they accepted the authority of female leaders. Dying without a son, Prasutagus had left his people in the care of his widow, Boadicea (or Boudicca), until their two daughters came of age.

But women had few rights under Roman law, and Nero's local officials treated Boadicea's succession with contempt.

'Kingdom and household alike,' wrote the Roman historian Tacitus, author of the first history of Britain, 'were plundered like prizes of war.'

The lands of the Iceni nobles were confiscated and Boadicea was publicly beaten. Worst of all, her two daughters were raped. Outraged, in AD 61 the Iceni rose in rebellion, and it was Boadicea who led them into battle.

'In stature she was very tall, in appearance most terrifying,' wrote a later Roman historian, Dio Cassius. 'Her glance was fierce, her voice harsh, a great mass of the most tawny hair cascaded to her hips.'

Joined by other Britons, Boadicea with her rebel Iceni fell on Colchester in fury, slaughtering the inhabitants and smashing the white-pillared temple and other symbols of Roman oppression. Over eighteen hundred years later, in 1907, a boy swimming in the River Alde in Suffolk, deep in what had been Iceni territory, was astonished to discover the submerged bronze head of the emperor Claudius. Looking at the jagged edges of the severed neck today, one can almost hear the shouts of anger that have attended the satisfying ritual of statue toppling over the centuries.

The rebels now turned towards Londinium, the trading settlement that was just growing up around the recently built bridge over the Thames. The vengeance they wreaked here was equally bitter. Today, four metres below the busy streets of the modern capital, near the Bank of England, lies a thick red band of fired clay and debris which archaeologists know as 'Boadicea's Layer'. The city to which the Iceni set the torch burned as intensely as it would in World War II during the firebomb raids of the Germans. Temperatures rose as high as 1000 degrees Celsius – and, not far away, in the Walbrook Stream that runs down to the Thames, has been found a grisly collection of skulls, violently hacked from their bodies.

Boadicea's forces had wiped out part of a Roman legion that had marched to the rescue of Colchester. But the bulk of the Roman troops had been on a mission in the north-west to hunt down the Druids and destroy their groves on the island of Anglesey, and it was a measure of Boadicea's self-assurance that she now headed her army in that north-westerly direction. Her spectacular victories had swollen her ranks, not only with warriors but with their families too, in a vast wagon train of women and children. She laid waste to the Roman settlement of Verulamium, modern St Albans, then moved confidently onwards.

Meanwhile the Romans had been gathering reinforcements and the two forces are thought to have met somewhere in the Midlands, probably near the village of Mancetter, just north of Coventry.

'I am fighting for my lost freedom, my bruised body and my outraged daughters!' cried Boadicea, as she rode in her chariot in front of her troops. 'Consider how many of you are fighting and why – then you will win this battle, or perish! That is what I, a woman, plan to do! Let the men live in slavery if they want to.'

These fighting words come from the pen of Tacitus, who describes the fierce showdown in which the much smaller, but impeccably armed and drilled Roman army wore down the hordes of Boadicea. At the crux of the battle, it was the wagon train of British women and children that proved their menfolk's undoing. The camp followers had fanned out in a semicircle to watch the battle, fully expecting another victory. But as the Britons were driven back, they found themselves hemmed in by their own wagons, and the slaughter was terrible – eighty thousand Britons killed, according to one report, and just four hundred Romans. Boadicea took poison rather than fall into the hands of the Romans, and, legend has it, gave poison to her daughters for the same reason.

It was only when some of Tacitus' writings, lost for many centuries, were rediscovered five hundred and fifty years ago that Britain found out that its history had featured this inspiring and epic warrior queen. Plays and poems were written to celebrate Boadicea's battle for her people's rights and liberties, and in 1902 a stirring statue in her honour was raised in the shadow of the Houses of Parliament. There on the banks of the Thames you can see Boadicea thrusting her spear defiantly into the air, while her daughters shelter in the chariot beside her.

But the menacing curved blades on Boadicea's chariot wheels are, sadly, the invention of a later time. Remains of the Britons' light bentwood chariots show no scythes on the wheels. Nor is there evidence of another great myth, that Boadicea fought her last battle near London and that her body lies where she fell – in the ground on which King's Cross Station was built many years later. Her supposed grave beneath platform ten at King's Cross is the reason why Harry Potter's Hogwarts Express leaves, magically, from Platform Nine and Three-Quarters.

In fact, the bones of the great queen probably do lie near

a railway line – albeit more than a hundred miles north of King's Cross, near Mancetter in modern Warwickshire. The trains on the Euston line between London and the north-west rumble through the battlefield where, historians calculate, Boadicea fought her last battle.

HADRIAN'S WALL

AD 122

THE ROMANS EXACTED FIERCE REVENGE FOR Boadicea's revolt. Reinforcements were sent over from Germany and, as Tacitus put it, 'hostile or wavering peoples were ravaged with fire and sword'.

But tempers cooled, and in AD 77 a new governor arrived in Britain, Gnaeus Julius Agricola. His daughter was married to the historian Tacitus and it seems likely that Tacitus himself came with his father-in-law and served on his staff for a while. So it was from first-hand observation that he described how Agricola, to promote peace, 'encouraged individuals and helped communities to build temples, market-places and houses. Further, he trained the sons of the chiefs in the liberal arts and expressed a preference for British natural ability.'

As a result, wrote the reporter-historian, 'the people, who used to reject the Latin language, began to aspire to being eloquent in it. Even the wearing of our Roman robes and togas came to be esteemed. And so, little by little, the Britons were seduced into alluring vices – colonnades, baths and elegant banquets.'

Then, as now, the well-to-do locals showed themselves suckers for Italian trendiness. Beautiful mosaics, underfloor heating, villas, law courts, council chambers, sports stadiums, bath-houses, amphitheatres, roads – handsome stone structures of all kinds sprang up in the main Roman settlements, especially in the south of the island. But the most massive construction project of all was the Empire's huge northern frontier wall, started in AD 122 and some six years in the building.

The great wall was the work of the emperor Hadrian, a patient and thorough man who spent half of his twenty-one-year reign systematically travelling the boundaries of his vast Empire, sorting out problems. In Britain, Rome's problem was the warlike peoples in the north of the island – the Picts and the Caledonians – whom the legions had found it impossible to subdue.

Running seventy-three miles from the River Tyne on the east coast to the Solway Firth on the west, Hadrian's Wall was 3 metres thick and 5 metres high, a huge stone-faced rampart with a succession of full-scale frontier forts along its length. In 143, Hadrian's successor Antoninus built another row of ditches and turf defences a hundred miles further north, and for as long as this, the Antonine Wall, held, it created a broad northern band of Roman-dominated territory.

Excavations show that Hadrian's Wall was a centre of bustling colonial life where soldiers and their families lived, traded and, to judge from the scraps of letters that survive, invited each other to dinner parties. To the rolling windswept hills of northern Britain the Romans brought *garum*, the dark, salty fish sauce that was the ketchup of the Roman legionary, poured over everything. For the sweet tooth there was *defrutum* – concentrated grape syrup that tasted like fruit squash. Another scrap of letter refers to the thermal socks and underwear that a Roman soldier needed to keep himself warm on the northern border.

It is not likely that many of Britain's border farmers wore togas or conversed in Latin. But they must have learned a few words as they haggled over the price of grain with the Roman quartermaster or bit on the coins that bore the current emperor's head. It was during Britain's Roman centuries that cabbages, peas, parsnips and turnips came to be cultivated in the British Isles. The Romans brought north bulkier, more meat-bearing strains of cattle, as well as apples, cherries, plums and walnuts for British orchards – plus lilies, roses, pansies and poppies to provide scent and colour for the island's early gardens. The British were famous for their trained hunting dogs, which they bred, trained and sold to Europe. But it was probably thanks to the Romans that now appeared, curled up by the second-century fireside, the domestic cat.

The Romans were proud of what they called *Pax Romana*, 'the Roman peace'. They cultivated the life of the city – *civitas* in Latin – the root of our word civilisation, connecting city to city with their superb, straight, stone and gravel roads. Some Britons joined the Roman army and were sent off to live in other parts of the Empire. Soldiers from the Balkans and southern Europe came to Britain, married local girls and helped create a mingled, cosmopolitan way of life. In AD 212 the emperor Caracalla granted full citizenship to all free men in the Empire, wherever they might live.

But the comforts of Roman civilisation depended on the protection of the tough, battle-ready legions that had built the Empire and now guarded its frontiers. Organised in units of a hundred (hence the title of their commanding officer, the centurion), Roman legionaries drilled every day – 'cutting down trees, carrying burdens, jumping over ditches, swimming in sea or river water, going on route marches at full pace, or even running fully armed and with packs,' as one fourth-century reporter described them. Could a modern SAS man emulate the crack Roman cavalrymen who had mastered the art of vaulting on to their horses' backs in full armour?

Those who remained outside the Empire were warriors too – and of them there were many more. The Romans called them *barbari*, from a Greek word that originally meant 'outsiders' but which came to be tinged with notions of savagery and fear. In AD 197, less than seventy years after its massive fortifications were completed, Hadrian's Wall was overrun by the Picts, the warlike barbarians of the north. Many of its forts had to be reconstructed.

A hundred years later southern Britain faced another threat. Sailing across from the low coastal islands of northern

Germany came the Angles and Saxons – pirates who preyed on the prosperous farms and villas of the south-east in lightning hit-and-run-and-row raids. In 285 the Romans started fortifying a line of defences and watchtowers to keep them at bay. Eventually the fortifications stretched all the way from Norfolk down to the mouth of the Thames and round the south coast to the Isle of Wight. The Romans called it the Saxon Shore.

But there was only so much that forts and soldiers could achieve. The pressures of peoples are hard to resist. The Angles, Saxons and other raiders from across the sea were part of the great swirlings of populations that were bringing change to every part of Europe. These barbarians – most of them Germanic peoples – penetrated the Empire willy-nilly, and by the early years of the fifth century they were sweeping southwards, threatening the survival of Rome itself. The legions were called home. In AD 410 the British asked the emperor Honorius for help against the continuing inroads of the seaborne raiders. But the bleak answer came back that from now on the inhabitants of Britannia must fend for themselves.

ARTHUR, ONCE AND
FUTURE KING

AD 410–c.600

'THE DARK AGES' IS THE LABEL HISTORIANS used to apply to the centuries after the legions left Britain. With the departure of the Romans, civilisation literally departed as well. If any written records of this time were made, virtually none has survived, and to this day we can only guess at exactly who did what to whom from 410 until nearly 600. Unlike Julius Caesar, the Anglo-Saxons did not keep invasion diaries.

What we do know for sure is that the Angles, Saxons and other peoples of northern Germany kept on rowing across the water to the white cliffs and sheltered harbours of Albion. Their poems tell of their brave exploits cresting the waves in their oar-powered, plank-built boats. Within a century and a half of the Romans' departure, the south-east corner of the island had indeed become the Saxon Shore. The newcomers had moved in and were busy creating their new kingdoms of Essex, Sussex and Wessex – the lands of the East, the South and West Saxons. They came, they saw, they settled.

The settlement extended widely. The Angles gave their name to East Anglia, and they founded more kingdoms up the coast – Lindsey (now Lincolnshire) and Northumbria, literally the land of the people north of the Humber, the wide estuary that separates modern Hull and Grimsby. In the Midlands lay the kingdom of Mercia, the people of the borders or boundaries. By the time this mosaic of little sovereignties was complete, the newcomers held most of the land.

But modern excavation has uncovered little evidence that this was a violent ethnic takeover. Hundreds of Roman villas and settlements have been dug up, with no severed skulls or suggestions of blood spilt on the tiles. No equivalent of Boadicea's fire-scorched layer has yet been found in what was becoming Anglo-Saxon England.

It would seem that most of the people who were left behind by the legions – the Romano-Britons – made some sort of peace, more or less grudging, with their new masters. Settlements along one river in Sussex show the Romano-Britons on one side and the Saxons on the other. The earliest law code of the West Saxons, drawn up by King Ine in the late seventh century, allowed the British who held land in his domain to keep some of their own customs.

It was further west and to the north that the violence occurred, in Cornwall, Wales and Scotland – the great crescent of sea, moors and mountains later called the Celtic fringe. Roman influence had been relatively slight here and the Celts had preserved their traditional identity. There is evidence of fortification and battles in these border areas, drawing a bitter boundary of blood and language between Celt and Anglo-Saxon. *Wælisc*, from which we get the word 'Welsh', was an Anglo-Saxon term applied to foreigners and also to slaves. And when the Welsh talk of England today they use a word that means 'the lost lands'.

It is from the so-called Dark Ages that some of Britain's most potent legends have sprung. As later chroniclers looked back, they pieced together scraps of memory and folklore – like the tales of the Saxon warriors Hengist ('the stallion') and Horsa ('the horse'), who were invited to Britain to help the locals and who then turned on their hosts. Did Hengist and Horsa really exist? The great modern expert on the subject was J. R. R. Tolkien, Professor of Anglo-Saxon at Oxford University from 1925 to 1945, who, having soaked up the atmosphere of these mysterious years, made up some legends of his own: Tolkien's tales of *The Hobbit* and *The Lord of the Rings* resound with the clash of swords in dark forests, where fantastical characters flit half-seen through a vanished landscape.

It took Tolkien twenty years to create his epic saga – 'saga' is the Norse word for 'tale' – but England's greatest Dark Age legend was generations in the making. In 1113 some French priests visiting Devon and Cornwall were astonished to be told of a great king – Arthur – who had once ruled over those parts and who would one day return from the grave to rule again. When the educated visitors laughed at the story, they found themselves pelted with vegetables by the irate locals.

The stirring legend of Arthur stems from fleeting references in a chronicle of around 829 – three or four centuries after he was supposed to have existed – attributed to a Welsh scholar called Nennius. There we read of a brave warrior who is said to have fought and won no less than twelve battles against the Saxons, and of that historical Arthur we know little more. But over the years, poets, painters, storytellers – and, in our own day, composers and filmmakers – have striven to embellish the Arthur of legend. Merlin, Guinevere, Sir Galahad, the Round Table, the Holy Grail, the Sword in the Stone and the Mists of Avalon were all later additions to the story. Tourist sites like Glastonbury, Tintagel, Winchester and the ancient hill fort of South Cadbury in Somerset have added their own local details as they have each staked their claim to having been Camelot, the seat of Arthur's court.

The legend of Arthur has struck a chord with every age, but his tale is strongly tinged with melancholy. Though chivalrous and brave, the King Arthur of poem and fable is defeated in his final battle, surrendering his sword, as he dies, to the Lady of the Lake. His knightly Round Table was overthrown, just as Romano-British culture was swamped by the new realities of the fifth and sixth centuries. So both in history and legend Arthur embodies a theme that has proved dear to patriotic hearts over the centuries – the heroic failure.

POPE GREGORY'S ANGELS

c.AD 575

IT IS EASY TO FORGET HOW MANY HAZARDS life held in previous centuries. Nowadays, if you get blood-poisoning from a bad tooth or an infected cut, you take antibiotics. In those days you died. For that reason, outright death in battle was almost preferable to the slow, agonising end that came with a gangrenous wound. And there was another battle hazard – if you were captured, you could well end up a slave.

Imagine yourself living in a village in the fifth or sixth century and seeing a strange boat coming up the river filled with armed men. You would run for the woods at once, for fear that you might be taken captive, never to see your family again. That's what happened to the young St Patrick, the son of a town councillor living on the west coast of Britain in the early fifth century. Kidnapped by raiders when he was sixteen, Patrick suffered six years of slavery in Ireland before he finally escaped.

Along the trade routes of Europe travelled merchants carrying with them the hot items for which the rich would pay good money – gold, jewels, wine, spices and slaves, a number of them captured in the battles between the Slavic peoples of the Balkans. The medieval Latin word *sclavus* ('captive') is the root of the modern words 'Slav' and 'slave'. In the principal European markets there was a corner where you could buy yourself a maidservant, a labourer, or even a scribe to take care of your writing and accounting chores. Teeth were inspected and limbs prodded by would-be purchasers, just as buyers today kick the tyres of cars.

It was in such a slave market in Rome that Abbot Gregory, a priest well known for his piety, was strolling one day around 575. Though Gregory had been born into a wealthy Roman family that owned slaves, he had sold off his estates to found monasteries and had become popular for his good deeds and his sense of humour – he had something of a weakness for wordplay and puns. Struck by the unusual appearance of a group of young captives with fair complexions and golden hair, he asked where they came from.

'From the island of Britain,' he was told, and specifically from the kingdom of Deira in Northumbria, the moorland area around the town of York, roughly equivalent to modern Yorkshire. At the mention of Deira, Gregory was tempted to one of his puns. In Latin, *de ira* means 'from wrath'.

'Then let us hope they will be rescued from wrath,' he said, 'and that they will be called to the mercy of Christ.'

But it was the news that these captives were Angles that inspired the pun that has been polished and repolished over the centuries. '*Non Angli sed angeli*,' Gregory is supposed to have said – 'They are not Angles, but angels.'

In fact, Gregory did not say that. His wordplay was more complicated. 'They have angelic faces,' he said in the most widely circulated version of this story, recorded about a hundred and fifty years later, 'and it is right that they should become joint heirs with the angels in heaven.' They might look like angels, in other words, but they were not angels yet. Christian conversion of these Anglish was called for.

Abbot Gregory, who became Pope Gregory I in 590, was a major figure in the growth of the Catholic Church. He is revered in Catholic and Greek Orthodox history as Gregory the Great – and, indeed, as a saint. His keen political sense and the popularity that he cultivated with the people of Rome contributed greatly to making the popes more than religious leaders. In due course the papacy would take over the city of Rome and would rule all of central Italy. Gregory also reformed the Church's services and rituals, giving his name to the solemn chanting inherited from Hebrew music, the 'Gregorian' chant or plainsong, whose haunting cadences could spread the faith across language barriers, making music possible without musical instruments.

But it is for his wordplay in the slave market that he is remembered in English history. The sight of the fair

Anglish captives in Rome inspired Pope Gregory to send missionaries northwards. He made history's pun come true – by giving the Angles (as well as the Saxons and the Britons) a chance to join the angels.

ST AUGUSTINE'S MAGIC

AD 597

IN THE HIGH SUMMER OF 597 POPE GREGORY'S missionaries landed on the Isle of Thanet in Kent bearing painted banners, silver crosses and holy relics. The man that Gregory had picked to lead the mission to the Angles was a trusted old colleague, Augustine – and his first target was cleverly chosen. King Ethelbert of Kent was a pagan, but his wife Bertha was a Christian, a Frankish princess who had brought her own chaplain from Paris. If Ethelbert was allowing his wife to practise her Christian faith in Canterbury, he must be a promising prospect for conversion.

Ethelbert greeted the missionaries with caution, insisting

that their first meeting should be out of doors – he did not want to be trapped by their alien magic.

'I cannot abandon the age-old beliefs that I have held,' he declared in his speech of welcome. 'But since you have travelled far, and I can see that you are sincere in your desire to share with us what you believe to be true and excellent, we will not harm you.'

In fact, the King let Augustine and his forty followers base themselves in Canterbury at an old church where Bertha worshipped – clear evidence that Christianity was by no means new to a country which had previously been a Roman province. Some time in the third century St Alban had become Britain's earliest saint and martyr when he suffered execution for protecting a Christian priest – and after the emperor Constantine was converted in 312, Christianity had been tolerated across the empire. But then the Anglo-Saxons had imported their pantheon of Germanic gods, a collection of very human deities inspired by storms, victory in battle and the forces of nature. The word 'pagan' comes from *pagus*, Latin for a country district and its inhabitants. When the Anglo-Saxon ploughman went out to cut his first furrow of the year, he would kneel and say a prayer as he buried a fertility cake baked from the last harvest's grain, asking the gods to allow the seed to germinate again.

Back in Rome, Pope Gregory had told Augustine to treat such pagan customs with respect. 'For in these days,' he explained, 'the Church corrects some things strictly and allows others out of leniency . . . By doing so she often succeeds in checking an evil of which she disapproves.'

The Pope wisely suggested that churches should be built

where the old pagan temples had been – 'in order that the people may the more familiarly resort to the places with which they have been accustomed'.

Rather than sacrifice to Mother Earth, the pagans were encouraged to pray to the mother of Jesus, the Virgin Mary. And our modern calendar shows the live-and-let-live inter-action between old and new: Sun-day and Moon-day were followed by Tiw's-day, Woden's-day, Thor's-day and Freya's-day, named after the Germanic gods of war, wisdom, thunder and love respectively. Saturn's-day was another pagan hang-over – from the Romans in pre-Christian times. The feast of Easter gets its name from Eastre, the Anglo-Saxon goddess of dawn and fertility.

As Ethelbert cannily studied Augustine and his compan-ions, he came to the conclusion that the Christians posed no threat to him. On the contrary, he liked what they had to offer – learning, piety, discipline, and a ready-made band of activists who were keen to go out and spread these solid virtues among his people. Augustine helped the king draw up the first Anglo-Saxon law code. The Christian magic was a potent and modern magic, and he had a special reason for urgency – Augustine and his missionaries warned all they met that the end of the world was nigh and that God's terri-ble judgement was at hand. Fourteen hundred years later we speak of the *early* Church, but Gregory, Augustine and their fellow-believers did not know they were only at the beginning of a very long story. They believed that time was short. Jesus could be coming back to earth at any moment – maybe that very night, 'like a thief', as he promised in the Bible – and King Ethelbert decided not to take the chance that these learned newcomers with their documents and paintings might be wrong.

Ethelbert was baptised, and he invited Augustine to make Canterbury the headquarters of his missionary efforts, giving him the land and money to build the first Canterbury Cathedral. To this day, Canterbury remains the headquarters of the Church of England, and Archbishops of Canterbury sit on the throne of St Augustine.

KING OSWY AND THE
CROWN OF THORNS

AD 664

AUGUSTINE AND HIS FOLLOWERS WERE NOT
the only missionaries at work converting the pagans of
Anglo-Saxon England in the years around AD 600. For
nearly half a century, Celtic monks from the island of Iona
off the shore of western Scotland had been travelling around,
preaching Christianity to the inhabitants of northern
England. Their teachings were inspired by the kidnapped
St Patrick (see p. 33), who, after escaping from slavery in
Ireland, could not rid himself of the 'cry of unbaptised children'. He had returned to convert his Irish captors – and,
according to legend, had also rid Ireland of snakes in the
process.

The graphic emblem of the Irish missionaries was the Celtic cross, the symbol of Christianity surrounded by a sunburst. Irish monks happily sought inspiration in Celtic culture, incorporating the sinuous geometric patterns of its imagery into their Christian manuscripts. They shaved the front of their heads in the tradition of the Druids and had their own date for Easter. So in the early seventh century England's patchwork of Anglo-Saxon kingdoms was being converted from two directions, with north and south practising Christianity in different ways.

The problem came to a head when King Oswy of Northumbria married Eanfled, a princess from Kent, who came north with her own chaplain and other followers. They practised their religion in the manner that Augustine had established – including the latest Roman way of calculating when Easter should fall. Christ had been crucified in Jerusalem as the Jews were gathering for the feast of Passover, so Easter's timing had to relate to the Jewish lunar calendar which ran from new moon to new moon in a cycle of 29½ days. But the Christian church used Rome's Julian calendar, which was based on the annual 365¼-day cycle of the sun – and whichever way you try, 29½ into 365¼ does not go.

'Such was the confusion in those days', related the historian Bede, 'that Easter was sometimes kept twice in one year, so that when the king [Oswy] had ended Lent and was keeping Easter, the queen [Eanfled] and her attendants were still fasting and keeping Palm Sunday.'

Oswy decided to call a conference to sort out this clash of timing and to resolve the whole range of differences between the rival bands of priests – among them the vexed question of the correct religious hairstyle, or tonsure. Down in the south clergy shaved a bald patch on the top of their heads, leaving a thin circle of hair all round the head just above the temples, in memory of Christ's crown of thorns. This was the Roman tonsure that contrasted with the Druid-like hairstyle of the Celtic monks, who shaved the front of their heads along a line going over the top of the scalp from ear to ear, with the hair behind their ears tumbling down in long, flowing and sometimes greasy locks. Not for the last time in English history, hairstyles were vivid and visible symbols of divided loyalties.

The two sets of holy men squared off at a synod, or church council, held in 664 at the Abbey of Whitby, high on a hill overlooking the rugged Yorkshire coast.

'Easter is observed by men of different nations and languages at one and the same time in Africa, Asia, Egypt, Greece, and throughout the world,' argued the Roman, southern English side. 'The only people who stupidly contend against the whole world are those Irishmen . . .'

'It is strange that you call us stupid,' retorted the Irish spokesman, citing the support of the gospel writer St John, and, more pertinently, St Columba, who had founded the great monastery of Iona from which so many of the Irish monks had come.

In the end it was the King who resolved the arguments. The Canterbury side had based their case on the authority of St Peter, who was believed to have brought Christianity to the city of Rome and to whom Jesus Christ had said, 'I will give unto thee the keys of the kingdom of heaven.' These words from the Bible impressed King Oswy mightily.

'I tell you,' said the King, 'if Peter is guardian of the gates of heaven, I shall not contradict him. Otherwise when I come to the gates of heaven, there may be no one to open them.'

Heaven and earth seemed very close in a world where life was so fragile. King Oswy plumped for the Roman Easter, the Roman tonsure and the overall authority of the Pope in Rome, tying England more firmly to the church's 'world headquarters', with Canterbury confirmed as the local 'head office'. The first reaction of the long-haired monks who had argued the Celtic case was to leave Northumbria disgruntled, returning to Iona and eventually to Ireland. There they discovered, however, that some Irish churches were already calculating Easter according to the latest Roman system – and the Roman tonsure eventually followed. In due course razors would shave the necks and scalps of all Irish monks in the Roman crown-of-thorns style.

Six years later, in 670, King Oswy, whose voice had been so decisive in Rome's victory, died as he was setting out on a pilgrimage to the Holy See of St Peter in Rome. His body was brought back to Whitby to be buried at the site of the historic synod by the sea, and if his spirit did manage to find its way to the gates of heaven, we must presume that St Peter was waiting there for him with the keys.

CAEDMON, THE FIRST
ENGLISH POET

C. AD 680

CAEDMON WAS A HERDSMAN WHO LOOKED
after the farm animals at the monastery of Whitby. His
Celtic name tells us he was of native British descent, like so
many others, as a labourer for the new Anglo-Saxon masters
of the land.

Caedmon was something of a dreamer – and very shy.
When guests gathered for the firelit evenings of song and
recitation with which the people of the time entertained
themselves he would shrink away when he saw the harp
heading in his direction. He would slip quietly back to his
home in the stables – and it was on one such evening, lying
down in the straw to sleep among the animals, that he had a
dream. The cowherd saw a man beside him.

'Caedmon,' said the stranger, 'sing me a song.'

'I don't know how to sing,' he replied. 'I left the feast because I cannot sing – that's why I'm here.'

'But you shall sing to me,' insisted the man.

'What shall I sing?' asked Caedmon.

'Sing the song of creation,' came the answer.

At once, in his dream, Caedmon found himself singing to God in a rush of poetry that he was astonished to hear coming from his own mouth – *'Nu scylun hergan, haefaenricaes uard'* – 'Now shall we praise the keeper of the kingdom of heaven.'

When he awoke next morning, Caedmon found that he could remember the whole verse from his dream, and that he could compose more. There and then he created an entire song, the 'Hymn of Creation'. He recited it that same morning to his boss the reeve – the manager of the abbey farm – who was so impressed that he took the cowherd along for a meeting with the head of the monastery, the abbess Hilda.

Hilda was a lively and welcoming woman. As Abbess of Whitby she had been hostess of the great synod that had argued over Easter and hairstyles some twenty years earlier, and now she gathered together a group of clerics to audition this cowherd who could sing. When they heard Caedmon's 'Hymn of Creation', the learned panel agreed that his gift of composing could only have come from God, and that the stranger in his dream must have been an angel. To test him, they picked out another theme, a story from the Bible, and next day he brought them more visionary verses that had come to him in the stable during the night.

Hilda was delighted. Caedmon should give up tending the cattle, she suggested. He must become a monk – and as the cowherd came to know the great stories of the Bible, so the inspiration flowed. He sang of the creation of the world, of how the human race had started and how the children of Israel had found themselves entering the Promised Land. He sang of Christ coming down to earth, of how God's son was crucified and then rose miraculously from the dead. And he also sang darker songs – warnings against the flames of hell and the terrors of the Last Judgement. Caedmon was like one of the cows that he used to tend, wrote a fellow-monk. He transformed everyday words into poetry, just as a cow, by chewing and ruminating, turns humble grass into green, fresh-smelling cud.

The cowherd stunned his listeners because his sacred verses were in the earthy language of ordinary people. By tradition, holy things had to be said in Latin, the language of the Church. In those days church services were all in Latin – as was the Bible. Speaking Latin was the sign of being educated and therefore superior. But now Caedmon was daring to sing hymns in Anglish, or *englisc*, the racy and rhythmic language of the Angles that was spreading across the island. *Englisc* was the language of the Anglo-Saxons' pagan sagas. In making poetry from the language of the less privileged, Caedmon, who died in the year 680, could be compared to a folksinger or even a modern rapper – and in Anglo-Saxon terms his 'Hymn of Creation' was certainly a popular hit. It survives as part of his story in no fewer than twenty-one hand-copied versions.

Every modern pop song bears a credit line – 'Copyright:

Lennon–McCartney', or whatever. Below the earliest surviving poem in English, composed one night in a stable on the edge of the Yorkshire moors, are written the words: 'Caedmon first sang this song.'

THE VENERABLE BEDE

AD 672/3-735

WE KNOW ABOUT CAEDMON THE COWHERD, Hilda the abbess, the Angles and the angels, and the insults that the Irish and English monks hurled at each other as they argued about hairstyles and the timing of Easter, thanks to the writings of the very first English historian, the Venerable Bede. To modern ears, it is a weird and even pompous-sounding name – 'venerable' meaning ancient and worthy, 'Bede' being an old word for prayer. But Bede the man was anything but pompous. He was a down-to-earth and rather humorous character – as you might expect of a Geordie lad, born in Northumbria near Monkwearmouth, now part of modern Sunderland. Bede spent most of his life in Jarrow on the banks of the River Tyne, where the modern Geordie accent, according to linguists, can be traced back to the Old English dialect spoken by Bede and his fellow-Northumbrians in Anglo-Saxon times.

The boy was just seven, and quite possibly an orphan, when he was handed into the care of the local monastery. In Anglo-Saxon England monks operated the only schools, and they trained their pupils in harsh conditions. In winter it was so cold in the Jarrow cloisters that pens slipped from the fingers of the priestly hands – while summer brought flies and infection. When plague struck the monastery in 685, the only survivors who could scratch up a choir were the twelve-year-old Bede and the old abbot, who managed to keep the services going between them, chanting and respond-ing to each other across the chapel.

Today there is a Bede Station on the Newcastle to South Shields line of the Tyne and Wear Metro. If you get off the train and walk past the oil tanks and electricity power lines of modern Jarrow you soon come to the very chapel where Bede and the abbot kept the singing alive thirteen hundred years ago. Sometimes there is only a thin curtain between the past and ourselves. In those days the Jarrow monastery was surrounded by green fields, and from its ruins you can get an idea of how Bede lived his life, studying and writing by candlelight for more than fifty years in his small stone cell.

He wrote with a sharpened goose quill that he dipped in acid. '*Encaustum*' was the monks' word for ink, from the same Latin word that gives us 'caustic', meaning 'biting' or 'burning'. Darkened with iron salts, Bede's ink literally bit into his writing surface, which was not paper but parchment – scraped animal skin. The parchment would have been stretched out initially on a wooden frame that prevented the skin from shrinking back into the shape of the lamb, calf or kid from which it came. It could take as many as five hundred calfskins to make one Bible.

On this primitive but very effective and durable surface, Bede worked magic. He wrote no less than sixty-eight books – commentaries on the Bible, a guide to spelling, works on science, the art of poetry, mathematics, astronomy, philosophy, grammar, the lives of Christian martyrs and a book of hymns. From his bright and simple Latin prose we get to know a man who was also interested in carpentry, music and the movement of the tides, which he studied and measured on long walks along the sands and rockpools of the blowy Northumbrian coast. Bede took a particular interest in cooking. He kept his own store of peppercorns, precious spices transported by traders from the other side of the world, to pound and sprinkle on the bland monastery food. He could be frank about the drawbacks of the monkish life. Writing of King Saul's two wives, he ruefully admitted: 'How can I comment on this who have not even been married to one?'

It is largely thanks to Bede that today we date our history from the birth of Christ – the AD method of dating that gets its name from the Latin *anno domini* ('in the year of our Lord'). The Romans had based their dating system on the accession dates of their emperors, but in his work *On the Reckoning of Time*, written in 725 AD, Bede took up the idea that the Church should not rely on this pagan system, particularly since it was the Romans who persecuted Christ. How much better to date the Christian era from the birth of Our Saviour himself! Six years later Bede put the system into practice when he wrote the book for which he is principally remembered – *The Ecclesiastical History of the English People.*

To this day, Bede's vivid narrative brings alive the texture of a turbulent time. He was a storytelling monk with a human touch, describing the terrible effects of famine in the land of the South Saxons where whole families, starving, would hold hands and jump off the white Sussex cliffs in tragic suicide pacts. In a credulous age he had a sceptical wit, poking fun, for example, at the legend that St Patrick had rid Ireland of snakes. This must mean, he wrote, that if any snakes happened to come over in a boat from Britain, they only had to inhale the scented Irish air to breathe their last.

This gentle dig at the Irish Christians reflected Bede's prejudices. He was English and proud of it. For him, the Angles and Saxons were God's chosen people, and his history tells us little about the Scots, and still less about the Welsh, of whom he disapproved heartily as troublesome heretics. He believed that life had a purpose, that men and women can shape their own destiny through hard work and faith – and for him that destiny was Christian and English.

But Bede's proudly local story contains scenes and ideas with which anyone could identify today. Imagine yourself among a group of Anglo-Saxon nobles discussing the pros and cons of the new Christian faith, when one of them comes up with this interpretation of life:

It seems to me that the life of man on earth is like the swift flight of a single sparrow through the banqueting hall where you are sitting at dinner on a winter's day with your captains and counsellors. In the midst there is a comforting fire to warm the hall. Outside, the storms of winter rain and snow are raging. This sparrow flies swiftly in through one window of the hall and out through another. While he is inside, the bird is safe from the winter storms, but after a few moments of comfort, he vanishes from sight into the wintry world from which he came. So, man appears on earth for a little while – but of what went before this life, or of what follows, we know nothing.

Bede's own sparrow flight across the hall of life was lengthy by Anglo-Saxon standards. He died when he was sixty-two, surrounded by his pupils, who were helping him finish his last work, a translation of the Gospel of St John into 'our language', that is, from Latin into *englisc*.

'Learn quickly now,' he told them, 'for I do not know how much longer I will live.'

He dictated the final chapter, then turned to one of his pupils. 'I have a few treasures in my little box,' he said. 'Run quickly and fetch the priests of our monastery, so I can distribute to them these little gifts which God has given me.'

And so, before he died, the Venerable Bede handed out to the monks his store of worldly treasures – some handkerchiefs, some incense and the remains of his beloved peppercorns.

ALFRED AND THE CAKES

AD 878

ANGLO-SAXON ENGLAND SOUNDS QUITE A cheery place, as described by the gentle and generous Bede from the security of his monastic cell. But we read of quite another country in the blood-drenched pagan sagas of the age. Winter howls. Ravens wheel over trees that are bent and blasted by the sea winds. Storms crash against rocky slopes. Darkness draws on. It was a perilous and threatening world that lay outside the torchlit circles of Anglo-Saxon settlements. No wonder their inhabitants declaimed courage-stirring poems of defiance of which the epic tale of Beowulf is an early example. Shepherds guarded their flocks against the wolf – 'grey ganger of the heath' – and long-tusked boar ran wild in the forests. Vast areas of the country were trackless watery wastelands.

These inaccessible brackish expanses were the main difference between the English countryside then and now. In East Anglia the Wash flowed into Middle England, a fenland of more than a thousand square miles where cattle had to be rounded up by boat. Half of Staffordshire consisted of peat and moss swamps, and much of the Thames Valley was a marsh. To the west lay the Somerset Levels, acre after misty acre of bullrush and sedge extending from Glastonbury to Bridgwater Bay. Pelicans, herons and the huge European crane took refuge in its wastes, along with fugitives and runaways – and, on one famous occasion, a king.

He was Alfred, King of the West Saxons, driven into the Somerset no man's land by the Vikings, the seaborne raiders who had started their attacks on England at the end of the previous century. They came from Denmark, Norway and the Baltic in their sleek and deadly longboats, crossing the North Sea as the Angles and Saxons had crossed it before them, pushed by the same pressures of population and attracted by easy pickings. One day around the year 800, the royal tax collector at Dorchester rode down to Portland to meet a fleet of Norse trading ships that had landed. But when he explained to the visitors how to pay their customs duties, they split his head open with a battle-axe. In the north the invaders captured and burgled the defenceless Abbey of Lindisfarne, drowning the old monks and taking away the young ones to sell as slaves.

The raids continued, decade after decade – and not just in England. In the course of the ninth century, Viking armies sacked Paris, Hamburg, Antwerp, Bordeaux and Seville. Moving fast in packs of five hundred or more, sometimes shouldering their lean-planked ships overland from river to river, the raiders even reached Russia – whose name comes from the Rus, the community of Vikings who set up their own kingdom in Novgorod, just south of the Gulf of Finland, in 852.

It was around this time that the Vikings in England adopted a worrying change of tactic: instead of returning home in the autumn, their armies started to settle. They took over the north of England, making York their own Danish-speaking, Danish-run capital, then extended their 'Danelaw', as the land they occupied came to be known, south into East Anglia, where in 870 they defeated Edmund, King of the East Angles. Refusing to renounce his Christian faith, King Edmund was tied to a tree and shot to death with arrows, according to one tradition. According to another, he was subjected to the inhuman Norse rite of 'carving the blood eagle', whereby the victim's ribs were cut away from his spine while alive. His lungs were then pulled out, to be spread like wings across his back. In the following century the martyred king's remains were moved to the Suffolk town of Bedricsworth, which in due course became a centre of worship and pilgrimage under the name of Bury St Edmunds.

Down in the south-west in Wessex, the last remaining centre of Anglo-Saxon resistance, King Alfred could certainly have expected a grisly end to match Edmund's. He was a devout Christian – he had travelled to Rome as a boy. When he succeeded his brother in 871, at the age of twenty-three, Alfred was more noted for his learning and piety than for warfare. His name meant 'elf wisdom', and while he did enjoy some success in battle his most successful tactic was to buy off the enemy. In return for payments later known as 'Danegeld', the Vikings would agree to go home for the winter.

But the next year they would reappear, and early in 878 an army led by the Danish king Guthrum drove Alfred westwards into the marshes of Somerset. It was Easter time and the King retreated with a small band of followers, dodging from islet to islet through the splashy bogs. They had nothing to live on except what they could forage from the local population – and from Alfred's desperate plight came one of the most famous tales of English history.

Taking shelter in the poor home of a swineherd whose wife was baking some bread, went the story, the refugee king was sitting by the fire, so preoccupied by his problems that he did not notice that the loaves were burning.

'Look here, man,' exclaimed the woman, who did not know that her bedraggled guest was the king, 'you hesitate to turn the loaves which you see to be burning, yet you're quite happy to eat them when they come warm from the oven!'

The endearing story ends with the apologetic king meekly submitting to the woman's scolding and setting to work to turn the bread; but the account does not, unfortunately, come down to us from Alfred's lifetime. The earliest manuscript that recounts the burning of the loaves (which turned into 'cakes' in the course of many subsequent retellings) was written about a hundred years after his death.

It is most likely a folk tale, handed on by word of mouth. Much was written about the heroic Alfred in the course of his life, and it seems surprising that such a very good story did not find its way on to parchment at the time. By the strictest laws of historical evidence, the story of Alfred and the cakes must be rated a myth.

But while myths may be factually untrue, they can help convey a deeper truth – in this case the humbling of the great king hiding in the marshes. So down-and-out that he had to suffer the scolding of a peasant woman, Alfred showed grace under pressure. He resisted the temptation to pull rank and lash out when rebuked – and he also made good use of his weeks in the wilderness. In May 878 Alfred rode out of his fortified camp in the marshes at Athelney, met up with his people and, just two days later, led them to a famous victory at Edington in Wiltshire. Guthrum was compelled to renounce his bloodthirsty Norse gods and to accept Christianity. He withdrew to the Danelaw with his forces, and for a dozen years the Vikings left Wessex largely in peace.

Alfred made good use of the respite. He built a defensive network of forts and fortified towns known as *burhs*, from which comes the modern word 'boroughs'. No one in Wessex was more than twenty miles from a *burh* where they could take refuge, and many of these military settlements later grew into towns. Taking on the Vikings at their own game, he designed and built a fleet of longships – in later centuries Alfred came to be described as the 'Father of the Royal Navy' – and he also reorganised his army. As the *Anglo-Saxon Chronicle* reported in 893, 'the king had divided his army in two, so that always half his men were at home and half out on service, except for those men who were to garrison the burhs'.

The *Anglo-Saxon Chronicle* was one of Alfred's great creations, a history of England up to his own reign, which then turned into a sort of yearly newspaper, regularly updated, recording that year's events in a forthright and sometimes quite critical fashion. The first updating was in the early 890s, and from then on monasteries around the country added their own instalments to a project that was one of the most remarkable of its kind in Europe. The *Chronicle* reported battles, famines, floods, political back-stabbing, triumphs and disasters in lively prose – not in Latin but in English, the language, as Alfred put it, 'that we can all understand'.

Alfred felt passionately that his kingdom must be educated. 'The saddest thing about any man,' he once wrote, 'is that he be ignorant, and the most exciting thing is that he knows.'

He put together a panel of scholars and started to learn Latin himself so that he could translate some of the great Latin texts into English. In a world without clocks, the King was anxious to work out the exact time of day, inventing a graduated candle on which the hours were marked off. Then he came up with the idea of a ventilated cow's-horn lantern to stop the candle blowing out.

When Alfred died in 899, Wessex was a thriving and dynamic kingdom, and it is not surprising that he should have become the only king in English history to be known in later centuries as 'the Great'. But he himself was modest about his achievements. He suffered as an adult from the agonies of swollen veins in and around the anus, the embarrassing complaint we call piles, along with other pains that baffled his doctors. These infirmities seem to have contributed to a strong sense of his own imperfections, and his account of his life ended on a tired and rueful note. Comparing his life to a house built out of whatever timber he could forage from the forests of experience, he described how 'in each tree I saw something that I required'. He advised others 'to go to the same woods where I have cut these timbers' so that they could construct their own house of life, 'with a fair enclosure and may dwell therein pleasantly and at their ease, winter and summer, as I have not yet done'.

Reading these words, it does seem reasonable to assume that such a spiritual and modest man would have accepted the reproof of a peasant woman when he let her loaves burn in the wilderness. But Alfred himself would surely expect us to be rigorous about the truth.

THE LADY OF THE MERCIANS

AD 911-18

THERE IS A BATTERED SILVER PENNY FROM KING Alfred's reign on which is inscribed the grand Latin title REX ANGLO[RUM] – 'King of the English'. But the claim was only half true. Alfred had been King of those *Angel-cynn*, the kin or family of the English, who lived in Wessex, and his resourcefulness had kept Englishness alive in the dark days when the Viking forces drove him and his people into the Somerset marshes. The work of extending Anglo-Saxon authority across the whole of Engla-lond, as it would come to be known, was done by Alfred's children and grand-children – and of these the most remarkable was his firstborn, his daughter Aethelflaed, whose exploits as a warrior and town-builder won her fame as the 'Lady of the Mercians'.

'In this year English and Danes fought at Tettenhall [near Wolverhampton], and the English took the victory,' reported the *Anglo-Saxon Chronicle* for 910. 'And the same year Aethelflaed built the stronghold at Bremsbyrig [Bromsberrow, near Hereford].'

Women exercised more power than we might imagine in the macho society of Anglo-Saxon England. The Old English word *hlaford*, 'lord', could apply equally to a man or a woman. The abbess Hilda of Whitby (Caedmon's mentor, p. 45), who was related to the royal families of both Northumbria and East Anglia, had been in charge of a so-called 'double house', where monks and nuns lived and worshipped side by side and where the men answered to the abbess, not the abbot.

The assets and chattels of any marriage were legally considered the property of both husband and wife, and wills of the time routinely describe landed estates owned by wealthy women who had supervised the management of many acres, giving orders to men working under them. King Alfred's will distinguished rather gracefully between the 'spear' and 'spindle' sides of his family. It was women's work to spin wool or flax with a carved wooden spindle and distaff, and the old king bequeathed more to his sons on the spear side than to his wife and daughters with their spindles. But he still presented Aethelflaed with one hundred pounds, a small fortune in tenth-century terms, along with a substantial royal estate.

Aethelflaed turned out to be an Anglo-Saxon Boadicea, for like Boadicea she was a warrior widow. Her husband Ethelred had ruled over Mercia, the Anglo-Saxon kingdom that had spread over most of the Midlands under the great King Offa in the late 700s. Extending from London and Gloucester up to Chester and Lincoln, Mercia formed a sort of buffer state between Wessex in the south and the Danelaw to the north and east, and the couple had made a good partnership, working hard to push back Danish power northwards. But Ethelred was sickly, and after his death in 911 Aethelflaed continued the work.

'In this year, by the Grace of God,' records the *Anglo-Saxon Chronicle* for 913, 'Aethelflaed Lady of the Mercians went with all the Mercians to Tamworth, and built the fortress there in early summer, and before the beginning of August, the one in Stafford.'

It does not seem likely that Aethelflaed fought in hand-to-hand combat. But we can imagine her standing behind the formidable shield wall of Saxon warriors, inspiring the loyalty of her men and winning the awed respect of her enemies. She campaigned in alliance with her brother Edward, their father's successor as King of Wessex, and together the brother and sister repulsed the Danes northwards to the River Humber, thereby regaining control of East Anglia and central England. To secure the territory they captured, they followed their father's policy of building fortified *burhs*.

Aethelflaed built ten of these walled communities at the rate of about two a year, and their sites can be traced today along the rolling green hills of the Welsh borderland and across into the Peak District. They show a shrewd eye for the lie of the land, both as defensive sites and as population centres. Chester, Stafford, Warwick and Runcorn all developed into successful towns – and as Aethelflaed built, she kept her armies advancing northwards. In the summer of 917 she captured the Viking stronghold of Derby, and the following year she took Leicester 'and the most part of the raiding-armies that belonged to it', according to the *Chronicle*. This was the prelude to a still more remarkable triumph: 'The York-folk had promised that they would be hers, with some of them granting by pledge or confirming with oaths.'

The Lady of the Mercians was on the point of receiving the homage of the great Viking capital of the north when she died, just twelve days before midsummer 918, a folk hero like her father Alfred. She had played out both of the roles that the Anglo-Saxons accorded to high-born women, those of 'peace-weaver' and 'shield-maiden', and her influence lived on after her death. Edward had had such respect for his tough and purposeful big sister that he had sent his eldest son Athelstan to be brought up by her – a fruitful apprenticeship in fortress-building, war and busy statecraft that also helped to get the young Wessex prince accepted as a prince of Mercia. After his father's death in 924, Athelstan was able to take control of both kingdoms.

Athelstan proved a powerful and assertive king, extending his rule to the north, west and south-west and becoming the first monarch who could truly claim to be King of all England. In his canny nation-building could be seen the skills of his grandfather Alfred and his father Edward, along with the fortitude of his remarkable aunt, tutor and foster-mother, the Lady of the Mercians.

ETHELRED THE UNREADY

AD 978–1016

ETHELRED THE UNREADY IS A FIGURE OF fun in English history. It is now considered old-fashioned to classify monarchs as good kings or bad kings, but by almost any measure Ethelred was a bad one. In 978 he inherited the rich and respected kingdom of Engla-lond that had been pulled together by Aethelflaed, Edward, Athelstan and the other descendants of his great-great-grandfather Alfred. By 1016 Ethelred had lost it all, from Northumbria down to Cornwall, in the course of a reign that made him a byword for folly, low cunning and incompetence.

Perhaps the one sphere in which he deserves some sympathy is his unfortunate nickname, a mistranslation of the gibe made after his death by chroniclers who dubbed him Ethelred 'Unred'. In fact, *unred* was an Old English word that meant 'ill-advised', and it made a rather clever pun on the meaning of Ethelred's name, 'of noble counsel', rendering Ethelred Unred 'the well-advised, ill-advised'.

In Anglo-Saxon 'ethel' (also spelt 'aethel') denoted someone well born or royal – hence the vast number of Ethel-related names, from Ethelbert to Aethelflaed. All the offspring of a king, down to his great grandchildren, were known as *aethelings* – 'throne-worthies' – and it was from this gene pool that the *aetheling* who seemed most qualified for the job was selected. It would be many years before the rule of primogeniture, whereby the king would be automatically succeeded by his eldest son, came to prevail. If the Anglo-Saxon *aetheling* system still operated today, it might be decided that Prince William was more qualified than Prince Charles to succeed the Queen.

Ethelred, however, did not become king through discussion or consensus. He owed his throne to murder. One day when he was only ten, his older half-brother Edward – his father's son by a previous wife – rode through the gates of Corfe Castle in Dorset to quench his thirst after an afternoon's hunting. The young Ethelred was staying in the castle with his mother, and out in the courtyard a quarrel developed between her followers and Edward. They handed him a drink, then stabbed him to death before he could dismount.

Did Ethelred, inside the castle, hear his half-brother hit the ground in the courtyard? His mother was suspected of inspiring the stabbing, but Ethelred never investigated the murder that handed the crown to him as a ten-year-old, and it cast a shadow of suspicion over his entire reign.

The great challenge facing England during Ethelred's years was a new round of Danish invasions. Having left the island in peace for decades, the Vikings now returned with more rapacious raiding parties than ever. In fact, the raids were so ferocious that the Anglo-Saxons inserted a prayer in their church services every Sunday imploring God to spare them from the terror of the invaders. Ethelred resorted to Alfred's time-honoured tactic of paying them off, but he failed to take advantage of the time the Danegeld payments gave him to strengthen and reorganise his defences. The King seemed devoid of leadership qualities.

'When the invaders were in the East,' recorded one of the scribes of the *Anglo-Saxon Chronicle* with ill concealed disgust, 'the English army was kept in the West, and when they were in the South, our army was in the North . . . If anything was then decided, it did not last even a month. Finally there was no leader who would collect an army, but each fled as best he could, and in the end no shire would even help the next.'

For many of their raids, the Danes got help from their kinsmen in northern France. In 912 the French Channel coast had fallen to the Norsemen – *Normanni* in medieval Latin – and the sheltered harbours of Normandy provided ideal staging-posts for the Danes as they raided the south coast of England. Ethelred complained to the Pope, who got Duke Richard of Normandy to promise to stop helping Danish longships that were hostile to England. To strengthen his links with the Normans, Ethelred later married Richard's young sister Emma.

But the invaders kept coming, and in 1002 Ethelred took

a desperate step: he ordered the massacre of all Danes living in England. It was a foolhardy and wretched measure that gave the excuse for some Anglo-Saxons to settle local scores – the community of Danes living in Oxford were burned to death in the church where they had taken shelter. But even Ethelred's massacre was incompetent. There is little evidence that this dreadful ethnic cleansing was widely carried out – with one exception. Among the Danes who were killed was Gunnhilda, the sister of Sweyn Forkbeard, the King of Denmark.

It was a fatal mistake. The following year Sweyn led a huge Danish army up the River Humber, to receive a warm welcome from the inhabitants of the Danelaw. He returned in 1006 and again in 1013, fighting a campaign that eventually gave him control of all of England. England became a Danish possession, and Ethelred fled into exile in Normandy.

History books usually conclude Ethelred's story with the confused fighting that consumed the years 1013-16, ending with the deaths of both Ethelred and his son Edmund Ironside. But one episode tends to be overlooked. Sweyn died in 1014, and in a desperate attempt to regain his throne Ethelred offered to turn over a new leaf. Harking back to the conditions that Danish communities demanded when giving their allegiance to English rulers, Ethelred negotiated a sort of contract with the leading Anglo-Saxon nobles and clerics.

It was the first recorded pact between an English ruler and his subjects. Ethelred promised that 'he would govern them more justly than he did before', reported the *Anglo-Saxon Chronicle*. The king parleyed a comeback deal whereby 'he would be a gracious lord to them, and would improve each of the things which they all hated'. In return the nobles and clergy agreed to obey him, 'and full friendship was secured with word and pledge on either side'.

This contract, which appears to have been sealed in writing, was one of several last-ditch measures to which Ethelred had been driven in his weakness. As his authority eroded he had turned for help to the council of great lords and bishops who traditionally gave advice to Anglo-Saxon kings, the *witan* (plural of the Old English *wita*, meaning 'wise man'). Ethelred had used the prestige of the *witan* to bolster his appeals for taxes, for a national day of prayer against the heathen Danes and even for a nationwide fast during which just water and herbs would be consumed.

None of these frantic steps saved him. Though Ethelred was allowed back to England, he died in April 1016, and following the death of his son Edmund later that year the throne of England passed to the Danes in the shape of Sweyn's warrior son, Canute (Cnut). But some good came of the disaster. The ineffectualness that had compelled Ethelred to enlist the *witan* and that had inspired his last-gasp promise of good behaviour helped sow the seeds of a notion that would be crucial for the future – that English kings must rule with the consent of their people.

ELMER THE FLYING MONK

C.AD 1010

ELMER WAS AN ENQUIRING YOUNG MONK who lived at Malmesbury Abbey, and who loved to gaze up at the stars. During the troubled early decades of the eleventh century, he would look to the heavens for signs and portents of things to come, but while many of his contemporaries were content to draw simple lessons of doom and disaster, Elmer gazed with a scientific eye. He noted that, if you were to live long enough, you could see a comet come round again in the sky.

Elmer applied his experimental mind to classical history, making a particular study of Daedalus, the mythical Athenian architect and engineer who was hired by King

Minos to build his sinister labyrinth in Crete. To preserve the secret of his maze, Minos then imprisoned Daedalus and his son Icarus, who only escaped by building themselves wings of feathers and wax. Their escape plan was working beautifully until Icarus, intoxicated by the joy of flying, flew too close to the sun, which melted the wax in his wings. The boy fell into the Aegean Sea below, where the island of Ikaria perpetuates his legend to this day.

Elmer decided to test the story of Daedalus by making wings for himself, then trying to fly from the tower of the abbey. In an age when Britain was still suffering Viking raids, many Saxon churches had high bell-towers, both to serve as a lookout and to sound the alarm. Whenever the Vikings captured a church, the bell was always the first thing they tore down. Its valuable metal could be beaten into high-quality swords and helmets – and anyway, to capture the Christians' unique sound was a triumph in its own right.

Modern aeronautic experts have recreated Elmer's flight, and they calculate that his launch platform must have been at least 18 metres high, which corresponds to the height of surviving Saxon church towers. They also presume that he built his paragliding equipment from willow or ash, the most lightweight and flexible of the woods available in the copses of the nearby Cotswolds. To complete his birdman outfit, the monk must have stretched parchment or thin cloth over the frame, which, we are told, he attached to both his arms and his feet. Today the ravens and jackdaws that live around Malmesbury Abbey can be seen soaring on the updrafts that blow up the hill between the church and the valley of the

River Avon, and Elmer may have tried to copy them as he leapt off the tower and glided down towards the river.

According to William of Malmesbury, the historian who recorded Elmer's feat in the following century, the monk managed a downward glide of some 200 metres before he landed – or, rather, crash-landed. He did catch a breeze from the top of the tower, but was surprised by the atmospheric turbulence and seems to have lost his nerve.

'What with the violence of the wind and the eddies and at the same time his consciousness of the temerity of the attempt,' related William, 'he faltered and fell, breaking and crippling both his legs.'

William of Malmesbury probably got his story from fellow-monks who had known Elmer in old age. The eleventh-century stargazer was the sort of character dismissed as mad in his lifetime, but later seen as a visionary. In his final years Elmer's limping figure was a familiar sight around the abbey – and the would-be birdman would explain the failure of his great enterprise with wry humour. It was his own fault, he would say. As William told it, 'He forgot to fit a tail on his hinder parts.'

KING CANUTE AND THE WAVES

AD 1016-35

KING CANUTE (CNUT) WHO RULED THE English from 1016 until 1035 and who tried to turn back the waves, has gone down in folklore as the very model of arrogance, stupidity and wishful thinking.

One day the King invited his nobles down to the beach as the tide was coming in, ordering his throne to be placed where the waves were advancing across the sands. 'You are subject to me,' he shouted out to the water, 'as the land on which I am sitting is mine . . . I command you, therefore, not to rise on to my land, nor to presume to wet the clothing or limbs of your master.'

Not surprisingly, the sea paid no attention. According to

the earliest surviving written version of the story, the tide kept on coming. The waves 'disrespectfully drenched the king's feet and shins', so he had to jump back to avoid getting wetter.

King Canute's soaked feet are a historical image to rival King Alfred's smoking cakes, and, as with the story of the cakes, we get our evidence not from an eyewitness but from a manuscript that was not written until about a hundred years later. In the case of Canute we can identify the story-teller precisely as Henry of Huntingdon, a country clergyman who lived on the edge of the Fens around 1130 and who wrote a *History of the English* in praise of 'this, the most celebrated of islands, formerly called Albion, later Britain, and now England'. An enthusiast for his local wetlands – 'beautiful to behold . . . green, with many woods and islands' – Henry compiled his history from other manuscript histories, most notably Bede and the *Anglo-Saxon Chronicle*, and from the personal memories of people who had lived through the great events.

Henry was a conscientious reporter. His account of his own times has a careful ring, and if I were putting money on it I would feel safer betting that Canute got his feet wet than that Alfred burned the cakes. History's mistake has been the belief that Canute really did think he could stop the waves – according to Henry, the King thought quite the opposite.

'Let all the world know,' cried Canute as he retreated from his throne and contemplated his wet feet, 'that the power of kings is empty and worthless!' He shouted at the waves, in other words, to convey the message that he was *not* as all-powerful as he might seem, and he embellished his point with an additional, religious, lesson. 'There is no king worthy of the name,' he proclaimed, 'save God by whose will heaven, earth and sea obey eternal laws.'

The King of Heaven was the king who mattered, was his second message; and after this episode on the beach, according to Henry of Huntingdon, Canute never wore his golden crown again, placing it instead atop a figure of Jesus Christ. This tallies exactly with what we know of Canute's entire reign. As the son of the Viking Sweyn Forkbeard who had ousted Ethelred the Unready, he was anxious to emphasise that his family had converted from paganism and was now Christian. He gave generous gifts to embellish the cathedrals at Winchester and Canterbury, and also donated royal estates to support the abbey at Bury where pilgrims were starting to pray to Edmund, the saintly king who had been so cruelly murdered by a previous generation of Danish invaders (see p. 55). It was a matter of reconciliation.

Canute was a battle-hardened Viking chief who had slaughtered mercilessly to secure his power. In later years he liked to take the helm of the royal ship, so he could steer himself when he was travelling along the Thames, and if you attended his court you were likely to be jostled by Icelandic bards ready to declaim the latest epic poem. In the course of his reign he took control of both Denmark and Norway, to create a huge North Sea empire that stretched from Greenland to the Baltic and from the White Sea off north-western Russia to the Isle of Wight. But Canute had a touching wish to be considered English. He always saw England as his power base, and he understood that the key to success there was reconciliation between Anglo-Saxon and Dane.

He achieved it. Realising he could not hope to control the whole of Engla-lond, Canute delegated his powers to trusted local governors, *jarls* in Danish, the origin of our word 'earl'. His reign saw the consolidation of England's counties and shires, with their own courts and administrators – the shire-reeves, or sheriffs. He produced a law code embodying the idea behind the contract to which Ethelred had agreed in the last moments of his reign: that a sort of bargain should exist between the King and his subjects. He wrote newsletters to the people of his adopted country, describing his personal impressions and feelings, for example, after a long trip when he had met the Pope in Rome.

'I have never spared,' he wrote, 'nor will I in the future spare, to devote myself to the well-being of my people.'

Canute was especially keen to discourage superstition, and anxious to educate those of his people who had not seen the light. For the sake of their souls he urged them to forsake their surviving pagan habits – the worship of trees, wizards and weather prophets, together with the magic charms that people offered up when they were trying to track down stolen cattle. Some of his laws sound barbaric today: 'If a woman during her husband's life commits adultery with another man,' read law 53, 'her legal husband is to have all her property, and she is to lose her nose and her ears.' But one hundred years later the comprehensive law code of Canute, with its respect for both Anglo-Saxon and Dane, was still regarded as an authority.

After the chaos of Ethelred's reign, this rough, tough Dane proved to be England's best king since Alfred – both wise and realistic. Realism was one of the lessons he was aiming to teach when he had tried to turn back the waves, and it is one of history's injustices that the monarch who took his throne down to the beach in order to spread wisdom has ended up looking an idiot.

EDWARD THE CONFESSOR

AD 1042–66

EDWARD THE CONFESSOR IS THE ONLY
English king to have been declared a saint by the Pope.
When people 'confess' anything nowadays, it is to actions they
are ashamed of – their mistakes, their sins and, perhaps even,
their crimes. If you hear someone say, 'I must confess', you
know there is some sort of an apology coming up. But in Old
English the word had an altogether more positive meaning.
Confessors were a particular category of saint who had not
been martyred but who had demonstrated their saintliness by
testifying actively to their faith – in the case of King Edward,
to the spiritual happiness that Christianity had brought to his
not-always happy life. He was Edward the Testifier.

King Edward's testifying took the form of the immense abbey that he constructed in the fields a mile or so to the west of the walled city of London – the west minster (or monastery church), as opposed to the east minster of St Paul's that was London's cathedral. The soaring grandeur of the Westminster Abbey that we know today reflects the reshaping of the building in later centuries. But Edward's original abbey was grand enough. Built of stone, nearly 100 metres long and towering above the banks of the Thames, it was the largest church – in fact, the largest building of any sort – in Anglo-Saxon England. Edward modelled his great minster on the impressive new Romanesque architecture of Normandy where he had spent most of his youth.

He had had a lonely childhood. He saw little of his parents, Ethelred the Unready and Emma, the Norman noblewoman whom Ethelred married in 1002 (see p. 66). Through most of his boyhood Edward's distracted father was busy with the losing battle that he was fighting against the Danes, and after Ethelred's death in 1016 and Canute's Danish conquest of England, the boy took refuge with his mother's relatives in Normandy.

Emma, however, did not join her eleven-year-old son in exile. Following the custom of conquerors, Canute secured his hold on his new kingdom by marrying the widow of his defeated enemy, and Emma seemed to enjoy the experience. In the eighteen years that she was married to Canute, she became so Danish it was as if she had never been married to Ethelred. When Canute died and Edward finally returned to England, his mother scarcely welcomed him. She had had a son by Canute, Hartha Canute, whom she preferred. So after

Hartha Canute died in 1042, clearing Edward's path to the throne, it was hardly surprising that once he had established his power the new king rounded up his earls, rode to Winchester where his mother was living, and confiscated all her treasure.

By now Edward was thirty-seven. He was a tall, skinny man with blond or prematurely white hair. Some later accounts suggest that he may have been lacking in normal pigmentation in skin, hair and eyes – an albino. One description hints at a pale, almost translucent complexion, so that the blood vessels in his cheeks would show bright pink beneath his skin. Looking otherworldly, speaking Norman French and spending much of his time at prayer, the Confessor was something of an outsider among the hard men of Anglo-Saxon England – a choirboy in a den of gangsters.

Edward owed his throne to the consent of the three great earls who controlled the country – Siward of Northumbria, Leofric of Mercia and Godwin of Wessex. Their landholdings were such that they could dictate terms to someone like Edward who was, in many ways, a foreigner. Of the three powerbrokers Godwin was the wealthiest and most powerful. In gangster terms, he was the boss of bosses, and in 1045 he received the pay-off for his role as kingmaker: Edward married Godwin's daughter Edith, and gave her brother Harold the earldom of East Anglia.

Six years later, Edward rebelled against his minders. He ordered old Godwin, Harold and the rest of the Godwins into exile, and packed Edith off to a nunnery. But his independence was short-lived. While Earls Siward and Leofric had been happy to see the back of the scheming Godwins, they were rapidly antagonised by the pro-Norman policies that the King now adopted. Edward had spent most of his life among Normans. They were the people he really understood and trusted. So to his Norman nephew Ralf the Timid he gave large estates in Herefordshire, where Ralf started building a mini-Normandy, complete with castles.

Edward also worried the English with the favour he showed to his forceful and ambitious relative, William the Bastard. William was the son of Emma's nephew, Duke Robert of Normandy, and was known as 'the Bastard' because his father never married his mother Herlève, a tanner's daughter, whose beauty, according to later legend, was said to have caught Robert's eye while she was washing clothes, bare legged, in a stream. After his father's death, William built Normandy into a dynamic military power, displaying ambitions that many English found disturbing. It was rumoured that, out of gratitude for Norman hospitality during his days of exile, Edward had even promised this distant kinsman that he could inherit the English throne after his death.

When old Godwin and his son Harold sailed defiantly up the Thames the following summer, the fleet that Edward raised against them refused to fight. The confessor king was humiliated. He had no choice but to accept the restoration of Godwin power, which Harold wielded after his father's death in 1053. Harold now took his father's title as Earl of Wessex. Edward was also compelled to bring his wife Edith back to court from the nunnery, though it was rumoured that he refused to have sexual relations with her. The loveless marriage certainly proved to be childless, and Edith's family was denied the satisfaction of welcoming into the world an heir who was both royal *and* half Godwin.

With the return of the Godwins, Edward scaled down his bid to be an effective king. Delegating his military power to Harold, he took consolation in his beloved minster, to which he devoted a tenth of his royal income.

On the riverbank nearby he built himself a home, the Palace of Westminster – the site of today's Houses of Parliament; and he spent his days there, praying with his monks and reading the Bible.

Edward's saintliness was confirmed when he started laying his hands on sufferers from scrofula, a form of tuberculosis that causes swellings in the lymph glands of the neck. Victims believed that their swellings decreased after the king had touched them, and it became a tradition for English monarchs to lay their hands on sufferers from this disease, later known as the 'King's Evil'. The ceremony of kings and queens 'touching for the King's Evil' continued into the eighteenth century and the reign of Queen Anne, who touched the infant Dr Johnson in 1712, without effecting a cure.

Edward's great Abbey of Westminster became the spot where the English monarchy did its business with God, the place where every monarch would be crowned except the twentieth-century king, Edward VIII – Edward the Abdicator, as he would have been called in the Middle Ages. Many kings and queens were also buried there, to be joined over the centuries by the nation's non-royal headline-makers. In Poets' Corner lie the writers, beside a historic cavalcade of statesmen, soldiers, scientists and other heroes – with just a few heroines – in a marble forest of statues and tombs. The Confessor's abbey has become England's hall of fame.

Edward himself was too ill to attend the dedication of his minster when it was finally completed in December 1065, and a week later he was dead, leaving England up for grabs. Since the saintly Confessor had failed to produce any children, the succession came down to a contest between Godwin's son Harold and the Duke of Normandy, William the Bastard. Harold had no blood connection at all, and William had only a distant claim. But both men knew how to fight a good battle.

THE LEGEND OF LADY GODIVA

c. AD 1043

THE IDEA OF A BEAUTIFUL NAKED LADY riding her horse through the streets in broad daylight has an appeal that extends far beyond history. Today the name 'Godiva' is used as a trademark all over the world for striptease clubs and skimpy underwear, advertised by smiling young women with long, rippling hair. Yet these modern Godivas do not deploy their long hair to conceal their nakedness. On the contrary, they seem rather keen to reveal it – and they would certainly shock the pious Anglo-Saxon lady to whom they offer their naughty tribute.

The original Godiva was generous, kind-hearted and, by all accounts, highly respectable. In Anglo-Saxon her name was Godgifu, or 'God's gift'. She was a prominent figure in Edward the Confessor's England, owning large estates in her own right in the Midlands and East Anglia, and she was married to Leofric of Mercia, one of the three powerful earls who had placed Edward on the throne in 1042. Leofric effectively controlled most of central England, and he was selected by Edward to join the posse that raided the property of the King's mother Emma (see p. 79).

Godgifu and Leofric followed Edward's example of giving generously to the Church. Nowadays ambitious bigwigs buy the local football team and spend their money trying to help it to success. In the Middle Ages they showered their riches on the local church – or churches, in the case of Godgifu. In Coventry she devoted a great deal of her wealth to making its humble abbey the pride of the county of Warwickshire and beyond. 'There was not found in all England a monastery with such an abundance of gold and silver, gems, and costly garments,' wrote the chronicler Roger of Wendover in the early thirteenth century. And it was Roger who first wrote down the tale:

Longing to free the town of Coventry from the oppression of a heavy tax, Lady Godiva begged her husband with urgent prayers, for the sake of Jesus and his mother Mary, that he would free the town from the toll, and from all other heavy burdens. The earl rebuked her sharply. She was asking for something that would cost him much money, and he forbade her to raise the subject with him again. But, with a woman's persistence, she would not stop pestering her husband, until he finally gave her this reply. 'Mount your horse, and ride naked before all the people, through the market of the town, from one end to the other, and on your return you shall have your request.' To which Godiva replied, 'But will you give me permission if I am ready to do it?' 'I will,' her husband replied. Whereupon the countess, beloved of God, loosed her hair and let down her tresses, which covered the whole of her body like a veil. And then, mounting her horse, and attended by two knights, she rode through the market place, without being seen, except her fair legs. And having completed the journey, she returned with gladness to her astonished husband, and obtained of him what she had asked. Earl Leofric freed the town of Coventry and its inhabitants from the taxes.

So there you have the story, translated from the Latin that Roger scratched into his parchment around the year 1220 – and you will notice that, like Alfred's 'cakes' and Canute's waves, this colourful episode was not recorded until many years after it was supposed to have happened. Roger of Wendover's description of Lady Godgifu is rather like Trevor McDonald reporting on the Battle of Trafalgar. Long before Roger was born a number of historians had mentioned Godgifu in their chronicles, and not one of them had anything to say about naked horseback riding.

But there are several reasons for believing that Roger did not make the whole thing up. He was a monk at the Benedictine Abbey of St Albans, which had close links with the abbey founded in Coventry by Leofric and Godgifu. The monks went for prayer and study sessions at each other's abbeys, and their libraries exchanged manuscripts. So it is quite possible that the St Albans chronicler might have come across some since-vanished Coventry document that recounted Godgifu's stratagem for relieving the community's over-taxed poor.

Taxation was certainly a bitter and controversial local issue in 1043 when Leofric and Godgifu built their abbey at Coventry (a small part of which is now the site of the modern Coventry Cathedral). Just two years earlier feelings had been running so high in nearby Worcester that a couple of royal tax collectors had been set upon and murdered by the irate townsfolk. Leofric had been a commander of the army sent to discipline the community, and the brutal punishment he exacted involved ravaging the town for five days, before setting it alight and, according to the chronicler, John of Worcester, retiring 'with great booty'.

What did Godgifu think of her husband's role in slaughtering Worcester's tax protesters? It is tempting to wonder whether the 'gold and silver, gems, and costly garments' that she presented to her abbey two years later did not, perhaps, come from the booty of Worcester – Godgifu's own quiet way of making amends. But did her protest go as far as we have been led to believe?

In recent times, respectable members of the Women's Institute have stripped off so as to raise money for good causes, strategically placing apple pies and cookery books to substitute for Godiva's legendary long hair. But one cannot, sadly, imagine a grand and pious medieval lady doing any such thing. Godiva was one of the last great Anglo-Saxon women landowners. She inherited Leofric's vast estates after his death in 1057, and her possessions were listed in the Domesday Book. This God-fearing founder of monasteries and nunneries would hardly have ridden naked through rows of gawping peasants, however complete the camouflage of her luxuriant hair.

What does seem possible, however, is that Godiva may have ridden out *symbolically* naked – that is, stripped of the fine jewellery and sumptuous costume that denoted her status as one of the great of the land. Roger's source for the story may have used the Latin word *denudata*, which means 'stripped' – not necessarily total nudity. Maybe the jewels and fine outer clothes that Godiva took off for her ride were the very treasures that she was presenting to the abbey – and without fancy hairpins, of course, her hair would have come tumbling down voluptuously.

Symbolism was a powerful force in the Middle Ages. Riding penitentially through Coventry, an unadorned Lady Godiva would have made a forceful and startling statement by the standards of 1043. Her performance would have been well understood as a gesture of the sympathy she felt with the people of the community – which we should not, by the way, think of as much of a town. According to the Domesday Book, eleventh-century Coventry was scarcely a village: just sixty-nine families are listed as living there.

But real nudity is much more fun, and that is how the story has not just endured, but developed. As Coventry grew into a bustling centre of trade, the citizens became so proud of their naked lady that they started their own annual Godiva pageant, a saucy cut above the attractions of any other Midlands market town. An account of 1678 describes a Godiva procession that attracted tens of thousands of visitors, and it was around this time that another detail was added to the legend. According to the seventeenth-century version, the medieval villagers had shown their solidarity with Godiva's protest by staying indoors on the day of her ride, with their shutters decently closed so that she could pass by unobserved. No one, it seems, was so cheeky as to look out at her, with the single exception of a tailor called Thomas, who was promptly punished for his curiosity by being struck blind (or even struck dead, depending on the storyteller). And this is the origin of another English folk character–Peeping Tom.

THE YEAR OF THREE KINGS

AD 1066

A S EDWARD THE CONFESSOR LAY ON HIS
deathbed, too ill to attend the dedication of his beloved
west minster, he summoned Earl Harold of Wessex to his
side. Harold had no blood claim to the throne, but he was
Edward's brother-in-law. He had helped run England for a
dozen years and he was the candidate preferred by the other
Anglo-Saxon earls, so now the dying king named him as his
successor. That, at any rate, was the story according to
Harold, and on 6 January 1066, the day that Edward was
buried, he had himself crowned King of England.

The story was rather different according to William the
Bastard, Duke of Normandy, who thought the succession

was rightfully his through his French connections with the dead king. Out hunting in Normandy when the news of Harold's enthronement reached him, he was so angry that he could not speak. His followers kept their distance while the imperious Duke, in his wordless fury, kept tying and untying the fastenings on his cloak. (It is just a detail, but buttons and buttonholes had not been invented in 1066.)

William's view of events and of why he should succeed to the English throne was to be set out in a stupendous piece of graphic evidence and propaganda, the Bayeux Tapestry – a unique work of art and one of history's most remarkable documents. Stitched to the orders of William's half-brother, Bishop Odo, to decorate his new cathedral at Bayeux near the Normandy coast, the tapestry is a vast panorama, 50 centimetres high and over 70 metres long – the width of a football field. It features 37 buildings, 41 ships, 202 horses and no less than 626 characters, including lifelike images of Edward, William and Harold, who act out the drama in a wide-screen production of seventy-three picture sequences.

The tapestry tells us the Norman story, starting in England where Edward is still on the throne, and shows Earl Harold sitting proudly in his stirrups, a hunting hawk on his wrist, as he rides to set sail for France. Here the tapestry gives a comic-strip version of a journey that Harold probably made to Normandy in 1064, when he is thought to have sworn some sort of oath to William. Harold's supporters maintained that it was a simple pledge of friendship between the two strong men who controlled the different sides of the Channel.

The story according to William, however, was that

Harold's pledge involved much more than mere friendship. The tapestry shows Harold making a deeply serious oath of allegiance – we see his hands outstretched, and he is swearing on not just one, but two large boxes of holy relics. Later Norman chroniclers had no doubt that Harold had promised to support William's claim to the English throne once the Confessor was dead.

For nine centuries people have argued fiercely about what Harold did or did not promise. It hardly seems likely that the ambitious and dynamic earl would have sworn away a kingdom voluntarily, and if the oath had been forced out of him, then he clearly did not feel bound by it when he took over England on Edward's death. But we know from the tapestry what happened next: a flaming ball of fire, described by the *Anglo-Saxon Chronicle* as a 'hairy star', appeared in the heavens.

Modern astronomers have identified this hairy star as Halley's Comet, named after the seventeenth-century astronomer Sir Edmund Halley, who identified it when it passed over England in 1682. Elmer the flying monk saw the comet pass over England in both 989 and 1066, and realised that it was the same 'star' returning (see p. 69). Halley was able to work out the other dates when the comet's seventy-six-and-a-half-year-long circlings of the solar system would have brought it close to the earth – and April 1066 was one of those moments. But William of Normandy was certain that the hairy star was a sign of God's anger at Harold for breaking his oath, and it served as God's authorisation for the busy picture that soon follows on the tapestry – a tableau of Norman axemen chopping down trees and building an invasion fleet.

In England, meanwhile, Harold was trying to strengthen his position. His lover for many years had been the beautiful Edith Swan-Neck – they had had five sons and two daughters together. But to cement his power within the English aristocracy, Harold now arranged a marriage of convenience with Ealdgyth, the sister of two of the country's most powerful earls. Ealdgyth and her brothers were grandchildren of Leofric and Godgifu of Mercia. In other words, brave King Harold's legal wife, the last queen of Anglo-Saxon England, was the granddaughter of Lady Godiva.

Harold might have done better to foster his relationships within his own family. The previous autumn, with ghastly timing, he had fallen out with his fiery brother Tostig who had stalked off indignantly into exile. And in the summer of 1066 Harold learned that his brother had teamed up with Harald Hardraada, the King of Norway. Hardraada believed he had a claim on England through a treaty concluded by his father with Hartha Canute, and in September 1066 Harold heard that Tostig and Hardraada had landed their forces in Northumbria and had taken control of York.

Harold knew that William's fleet was poised on the other side of the Channel ready to sail at any moment, but he had no choice. He marched his army north, covering no less than 180 miles in four days and making such good time that he took the invaders by surprise. On 25 September, outside York, he won a fierce and brilliant battle at Stamford Bridge in which both Tostig and the King of Norway were killed. The remains of their army were driven back to their ships.

Harold's lightning triumph at Stamford Bridge was one of the great victories of early English history. His Saxon army could claim to be the nimblest and most lethal fighting force in Europe. But just three days later, on 28 September 1066, William of Normandy landed with his troops in Sussex, and when Harold received the news he knew he had to march south at once. He reached London, again in record time, picked up reinforcements and proceeded towards Hastings, where William had established his headquarters. Harold and the English army took up their position on the ridge above the valley of Sandlake, or Senlac, just north of Hastings, at the spot now known as Battle.

The Bayeux Tapestry shows the Norman knights riding their horses into battle on the morning of Saturday, 14 October. In modern movies Norman soldiers, who are usually depicted as 'baddies', are identified by the sinister long, flat nose-guards that project downwards from their pointed, dome-shaped helmets. In fact, both sides at Hastings wore these helmets, along with chainmail armour, and they are both shown carrying the same long, kite-shaped shields.

One thing that does distinguish Saxon from Norman is their haircuts: the Anglo-Saxons are shown with long hair and with even longer droopy moustaches, while the Normans are moustacheless and are coiffed in 'short back and sides' mode, the backs of their necks shaved bare to the crown of the heads. This gave them an advantage in hand-to-hand fighting – they could not be grabbed by their hair or moustaches.

The more significant difference is that the Normans are shown fighting from horseback, while the Anglo-Saxons are fighting on foot. Harold's army did have horses – they rode them to the battle. But then they tethered them and found they were facing the formidable cavalry that William had shipped over the Channel. The Normans had bred themselves a compact and powerful warhorse, the destrier, whose arched neck and small head indicate that it may have had Arab blood, and this battle-bred charger would play a crucial role at Hastings.

The Norman cavalry rode powerfully out of Senlac valley, casting their javelins into the Anglo-Saxon shield wall, then retreating. The battle wavered both ways, and there were moments when it seemed that victory could be Harold's. But the English had not regained their strength after their extraordinary forced marches to Stamford Bridge and back, and now they were worn down by the charges of the Norman horsemen. Armchair generals have criticised Harold for the speed with which he rushed south to confront the Normans, staking all on his stand north of Hastings. He could have held back closer to London, it has been argued, thereby regaining energy and forcing William to come to him.

But dash and courage were always Harold's way, and as the sun went down the Norman army found itself master of the field. Lasting more than six hours, the Battle of Hastings was one of the longest-recorded military encounters of the Middle Ages, and its outcome changed the course of English history. England became Norman. Duke William of Normandy became England's third king in the tumultuous year 1066. And his defeated enemy, Harold, lay dead on the battlefield, slain by an arrow to the eye. Or so we have always thought . . .

THE DEATH OF BRAVE
KING HAROLD

AD 1066

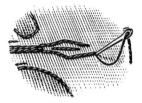

THE IMAGE OF THE LAST ANGLO-SAXON king on the hill above Senlac, staggering back tragically with a Norman arrow through his eye, has come to epitomise the drama of the Battle of Hastings. It is graphically depicted on the Bayeux Tapestry – but in this instance Bishop Odo's epic is not quite the reliable witness that it seems. Over its long nine centuries of existence, the tapestry has been hidden, stolen, damaged, restored, and finally displayed as a money-spinning tourist attraction. The stitching we see today is not always the original – and, indeed, some of it might be described as a stitch-up.

In 1729, when the tapestry was already over six centuries

old, a French artist, Antoine Benoît, carried out a full-scale tracing to serve as the basis for a set of engravings to be sold in France. Nearly a hundred years later, the Society of Antiquaries sent over an English artist, Charles Stothard, to prepare another series of facsimile prints. Then came the age of the camera, and the newly founded Victoria and Albert Museum in London despatched a photographer to make a photographic record of the tapestry. So we have three sets of images, dating from 1729, 1819 and 1872 showing how it looked in the past at three different points – and there are some dramatic variations.

Two British historians, David Hill and John McSween, have recently compared the three versions and have discovered no less than 379 differences. Swords and stirrups appear and disappear. A griffin becomes an angel. A horse that was a mare in 1729 has by 1819 become a stallion. Freckles – or maybe acne – appear on a Norman shipbuilder's face as a result of some creative darning. Three shields become two, and fish turn into seals. Continuity seems to have gone by the board.

The most significant differences are in the successive depictions of Harold's slaying. In 1729 the King is grasping at the shaft of a spear that he could be trying to throw – or might, alternatively, be pulling out of his forehead. In 1819 the shaft has sprouted feathers, to become an arrow pointing towards his forehead. But fifty-three years later, in the photograph of 1872, the angle of the arrow has shifted downwards: now it is pointing directly into the King's right eye, which is hidden from us by the nose-piece of his helmet. This is what you see if you visit Bayeux today.

The reason for this literal re-embroidering of history lies with the industrious ladies of Bayeux. It is thought that the original embroiderers of the tapestry were English, working at Canterbury in the early 1070s to the orders of Bishop Odo of Bayeux. But once the tapestry crossed the Channel to France it was cared for by local seamstresses – among them, from the nineteenth century onwards, the chambermaids of the town's principal hotel. This was appropriate since the tapestry had become Bayeux's main tourist attraction, and the chambermaids seem to have made sure that it showed visitors the romantic picture they expected.

The earliest version of the arrow-in-the-eye story has been found in an Italian chronicle written by 1080, but the more likely account of Harold's death, written only the year after Hastings, is less romantic. According to the 'Song of the Battle of Hastings' by Guy, bishop of the French town of Amiens, the crucial moment came when the Normans finally broke through the Saxon shield wall that fateful Saturday afternoon. With Harold and a few of his retainers still holding out, William handpicked a hit squad to go off and kill the King.

The Duke had once boasted that he would meet Harold in single combat. But now he was taking no chances. Four Norman knights tracked Harold down and overpowered him, the first striking him in the breast, the second cutting off his head, and the third running a lance through his belly to disembowel him. According to Guy of Amiens, the fourth knight then performed the difficult operation of hacking off one of the dead king's legs.

Now the story gets even more gruesome. A poignant

tradition originating at Waltham Abbey in Essex, where Harold's tomb lies, describes the lovely Edith Swan-Neck picking her way through the heaps of corpses and eventually discovering the dead king's remains. They were so horribly mutilated that Edith alone could identify them as Harold's, 'by certain marks on the body, known only to her'. The standard battlefield mutilation that accompanied beheading and disembowelling was full castration – chopping off the penis as well as the testicles – so Bishop Guy was almost certainly being polite when he wrote of a severed 'leg'.

That ugly interpretation seems borne out by the reported reaction of Duke William when he found out what had happened. According to William of Malmesbury, he was both furious and horrified at the final shaming detail of the assault on Harold, demanding to know who had carried it out. When he discovered the culprit, he promptly stripped him of his knighthood and sent him home in disgrace. Ruthless warrior though he was, William evidently felt that this atrocity had dishonoured his victory.

Posterity has agreed with him. In the last analysis, we cannot be sure whether Harold was shot through the eye with an arrow or dismembered by a hit squad of Norman thugs. It is, of course, possible that both calamities befell him, one after the other. But over the centuries people have tended to nurture the less horrendous version of events. The Norman Conquest was a disaster for Anglo-Saxon society, a bitter defeat that involved subjugation, famine, ethnic atrocities and humiliation – it was one of the most brutal times in English history, in fact. After such a trauma it is natural for a community to look for some sort of healing, and re-embroidering history can go some way towards achieving it.

The Bayeux Tapestry gives us over 70 metres of proof that history can be just about anything you care to make it – or 64.45 metres, according to the Nazi historians who examined its slightly shrunken form after it had been taken down for safety during the Second World War. In 1940 German forces had occupied Normandy along with the rest of northern France, and as Hitler prepared to invade England a team of scholars were despatched to Bayeux. After all, the famous tapestry depicted the last successful cross-Channel invasion, and the academics were commissioned to investigate what lessons might be learned.

They sent back an encouraging report to Hitler's henchman Heinrich Himmler, head of the German secret police, the Gestapo, and founder of the SS. The decorative animals woven into the tapestry's borders derived from German mythology, they stated. Better still, the whole message of the saga symbolised three 'characteristic German traits . . . the joy of fighting, the love of war, and the chivalric respect of the enemy'. So this Norman tapestry that had been woven in England, they concluded, was actually 'a sort of German royal saga'. Heil Hitler!

HEREWARD THE WAKE AND THE
NORMAN YOKE

AD 1070

WITH HIS VICTORY AT HASTINGS, WILLIAM the Bastard became William the Conqueror, and he staged his crowning as King William I of England in the Confessor's great abbey on Christmas Day 1066. In terms of the law and of blood descent the Duke of Normandy knew that his claim to the throne was slight, so he introduced a new element into the Anglo-Saxon coronation ceremony – a call for the people's consent to his rule. Questioned in both English and French as to whether they freely accepted William as their lord, the assembled congregation obediently burst into shouts of '*Vivat Rex!*' – 'Long live the King!' But outside the abbey, William's guard of Norman knights misinterpreted the pandemonium. Maybe they panicked, or maybe they wanted an excuse to panic. The mounted warriors went on a rampage, setting fire to the surrounding buildings and slaughtering any Saxon not quick enough to get out of their way.

England's first Norman king might have asked for popular consent inside Westminster Abbey, but the burned houses nearby made it clear that the Conqueror was well named – his power rested on force of arms. William's first project in the New Year was to throw up a wooden fortress on the banks of the Thames, the original Tower of London. The new arrival wished to make clear who England's new boss was, and castles became the trademark of his reign. The weathered stone towers and battlements of Norman England remain romantic landmarks to this day. But they were anything but romantic to the Anglo-Saxons who were conscripted to dig the ditches for the moats, raise and ram solid the great mound of earth on which the central fort would stand, then live the rest of their lives with the fortifications towering above them.

In the twenty-one years of his reign, William and his followers built hundreds of castles. Wherever there was trouble or discontent, the Normans rode in on their destriers, taught the agitators a lesson, then raised a castle to make sure it did not happen again. They built in wood to start with, throwing up pallisades of sharpened stakes that were replaced with stone in later years. And if a community had been particularly irksome, the castle would be built on the site of Saxon homes that had been trashed.

There is some evidence that William's original intent was

to be conciliatory. He tried to learn some English, and for several years he kept most of the local English sheriffs in place. The new king's early official documents bear the names of senior Anglo-Saxon office-holders, still in positions of high trust at court. But when William went home to Normandy in 1067 to check on the affairs of his duchy, a series of uprisings broke out. Three of Harold's sons by Edith Swan-Neck tried to raise Devon and Cornwall in revolt. Danish raiding parties sailing up the east coast found themselves being welcomed by the anti-Norman locals. The north rose, and Mercians on the Welsh border joined forces with the ever-defiant Welsh.

It was time to take off the kid gloves. Back in England, criss-crossing the Midlands and the north with his armies, William mercilessly punished neighbourhoods that had risen against him. Villages were destroyed and the country-side burned so that it remained derelict and uninhabited for years. Scorched earth, ethnic cleansing – all the horror words apply. It was a time of famine and tears that seared itself on the folk memory as the tyranny of the 'Norman Yoke'.

Just one centre of resistance held out. In the tradition of King Alfred, it was only in the Fens, in England's watery wastelands of treacherous swamp and brackish lagoons, that some local defiance survived. Hereward of Peterborough, a Saxon gentleman who had been deprived of his lands by the Normans, retreated into the East Anglian marshes around Ely with a band of fellow freedom fighters.

For a time Hereward received help from the Danish raiders in the area – and in 1070 he joined forces with them to plunder the Abbey of Peterborough. But when William bought the Danes off, the English kept on fighting. Hereward's guerrilla warfare became the symbol of native resistance. As the Saxon squire used the mists and marshes of the Fens to outwit his lumbering enemy, folk tales multiplied of his bravery and cunning, and of his legendary sword, which he nicknamed 'Brainbiter'. The folk hero gained a nickname of his own, Hereward the Wake – ever alert, luminous, elusive, the enduring Saxon embodiment of the fight for justice.

Not every Anglo-Saxon was impressed with Hereward. The monk who compiled the Peterborough version of the *Anglo-Saxon Chronicle* was scathing that an Englishman should help the Danes plunder the treasures of his local abbey with the excuse of denying it to the Normans – 'they said they did it,' he wrote sarcastically, 'out of loyalty to this minster'. The sacrilege prompted William to take action. Refusing to be defeated in the Fens by mere pools of water, the Normans built siege causeways – bridges of wood and earth embankments whose traces can still be found today in villages around Ely – and they flushed out the resistance. 'The outlaws all came to hand,' reported the *Chronicle* – with the exception of Hereward who, spry and nippy as ever, masterminded an escape.

What happened next is a mystery. According to one tradition, King William forgave the outlaw on account of his gallantry. That does not sound like the Conqueror, particularly after resistance that had cost him such expense and difficulty. The alternative story has Hereward betrayed into the hands of cowardly Norman assassins who stabbed him in the back with their lances. Either way, the Wake passed rapidly from history into legend. We do not know how long he lived or how he died, but within a generation or so the tales about him had been gathered into a Latin story book entitled *Gesta Herwardi Incliti Exulis et Militis* – 'The Exploits of Hereward the Celebrated Outlaw and Soldier'.

Starting from a grain of truth, the *Gesta Herwardi* expanded into yarns of wild fantasy that seem to have found a wide audience among both Normans and Saxons, many of whom would have listened to the tales as they were read aloud in Latin, or retold in instant translation. The plot lines followed some eternal stereotypes. In one exciting episode, Hereward returns to his family home to discover it full of Normans, with the head of his younger brother stuck on a pole beside the gate. In the style of Ulysses – or indeed of Ratty, Mole and Badger when they recapture Toad Hall from the wicked weasels and stoats – Hereward sneaks back into the house that night while the Normans are celebrating, and takes them by surprise. With the aid of just one follower, he kills the new lord and fifteen of his companions, cuts off *their* heads, and sticks them all up on poles where he found his brother's.

This was adventure fiction at its best – sheer wish fulfilment. But it was nonetheless popular for that, one imagines, when recounted around the firesides of the Anglo-Saxons.

THE DOMESDAY BOOK

AD 1086

BY 1085 WILLIAM THE CONQUEROR WAS nearly sixty, and he had long since settled into an annual routine. When he was in England he usually spent Easter at Winchester, the old capital of Wessex, which remained his working headquarters. For the Whitsun holiday he went to London, already the hub of English trade and on its way to becoming the country's capital; and he liked to celebrate Christmas in Gloucester, the old Mercian settlement on the border of Wales. William had ruled England for the best part of twenty years, and now, around New Year's Day 1086, it was time to take stock. Let the *Anglo-Saxon Chronicle* take up the story:

The king had much thought and very deep discussion with his council about this country – how it was settled, and with what kind of people. Then he sent his men all over England, into every shire, and had them find out how many hides [units of land] there were in the shire, or what land and cattle the king himself had in the country, or what dues [tax] he ought to have each year.

The Norman Conquest has been described in today's terms as a 'corporate takeover'. Twenty to thirty thousand Normans, a comparatively small number, became the new managers and controllers of the two million or so Anglo-Saxons and Danes who inhabited England. Modern managers take over a company's accounting system. The Normans took over the land – and now William wanted to know 'what or how much everyone who was in England had'.

The result of this countrywide investigation was the Domesday Book, so nicknamed by the native English as a sort of put-down, a resentful joke. William's great survey invaded everyone's lives, winkling out their secrets, they complained. Like God's Day of Judgement, it left people helpless in the face of such total knowledge, with no hope of appeal.

The book contained nine hundred pages of hand-written Latin – some two million words – describing more than thirteen thousand places in England and some parts of Wales, all examined in the most extraordinary detail. 'So very strictly did [William] have it investigated,' wrote the *Anglo-Saxon Chronicle*, 'that not a yard of land, nor indeed one ox nor one cow nor one pig was left out.' Leaving us in no doubt about their Anglo-Saxon origins, the monks added a sarcastic footnote: 'Shame it is to relate, but it seemed no shame to him to do.'

These critical monks understood the bottom line. Domesday was all about control and money. William had taken possession of all England, every square inch of it. As far back as anyone could remember, the Anglo-Saxons had held and farmed their land in a variety of ways. But now nobody owned land without obligations to the King: they held it as William's tenant, and had to pay for the privilege with 'service', which could take the form of a basket of eggs, some chickens, bacon, honey, a barrel of herrings, money, or supplying armed soldiers when the King called for war.

Many centuries later this system became known as 'feudalism', from the medieval Latin *feudum*, meaning 'fee' or 'payment'. The economist Adam Smith first coined the phrase the 'feudal system' in 1776 – long after feudalism itself was dead – and it has been talked about in high-flown, almost philosophical terms. In practice, it was the crude means whereby William and the Normans shared out England among themselves. It was a land-grab. Domesday makes clear that by 1087 all the major landholders were Normans or French – the original group of investors. The Anglo-Saxons had been cut out of the picture. If they held land at all it was as tenants to the invaders.

It is now more than nine hundred years since the English experienced subjugation: taking orders from people who don't speak your language, being forced to pay for land you thought you owned, and probably having some of your relatives killed into the bargain. There was one law for the

Normans and another for the natives. William's laws gave special protection to 'all the men I have brought with me, or who have come after me'.

This legal discrimination is reflected in the language that we speak today, a mixture of Anglo-Saxon or *englisc,* and Norman French. Our modern English words of control and authority – 'order', 'police', 'court', 'judge', 'trial', 'sentence', 'prison', 'punishment', 'execution' – all come from Norman French. And there is a similar linguistic apartheid in the way we describe food. When it came to the hard work of rearing and tending the animals, the words used were English – cow (*cū*), pig (*pigge*), sheep (*scēap*). When it came to eating them, they were French – beef (*bœuf*), pork (*porc*), mutton (*mouton*). It is not hard to see who produced the fruits of the earth, and who enjoyed them.

You can see the Domesday Book today in the airy glass and concrete National Archives building in Kew in south-west London. It is England's oldest public record, and anyone can go and look at it. The first known legal dispute that used the great document as evidence occurred in the 1090s, almost as soon as it was completed, and Domesday still has legal authority when it comes to the ownership of English land. For centuries it was kept in a rat-proof iron chest. Now it is carefully preserved, in four volumes, in an air-conditioned, shatterproof glass case.

The parchment looks soft, almost pinkish, the ink faded to brown with people's names picked out in rusty red. Here is Leofgyth, a Saxon woman of Knook in Wiltshire, 'who made and still makes gold embroideries for the king and queen'. We can trace the size of the estates that Godgifu,

Lady Godiva, owned in Worcestershire at the beginning of January 1066, 'the day King Edward lived and died'. And here are the details of the land held by the troublesome Hereward before he fled in 1071.

The Domesday Book is living history. To start with, the massive survey was known as 'The King's Roll' or 'The Winchester Book', reflecting where it was made and stored. But within less than a century it had come to be known officially by its rude English nickname, and has remained so ever since. The Anglo-Saxons might have lost the land for the time being, but they had the last word on it.

THE MYSTERIOUS DEATH OF
WILLIAM RUFUS

AD 1100

KING WILLIAM I DIED AS HE HAD LIVED –
a-conquering. In the high summer of 1087 he led his
troops to punish the town of Mantes on the River Seine,
which had dared to send a raiding party into Norman territory. As the Normans torched Mantes, some burning object
caused William's horse to rear up in fright. Now sixty years
old, the Conqueror was grossly overweight, and as his horse
lurched backwards the high pommel at the front of his
battle-saddle was driven into his soft belly, puncturing
his intestines. Bleeding internally, the King was carried
away to die, and as the priests gathered round him he set
about disposing of his empire.

William had three sons, and he didn't think much of any of them. Ridiculing the short stature of his eldest, Robert, he had nicknamed him 'Curthose' (Short-stockings) or 'Jamberons' (Stubby-legs), and he had not been on speaking terms with him for years. William saw no way of preventing Robert becoming Duke of Normandy, because of the Norman rule of primogeniture. But for England he picked his second son, William Rufus, and from his deathbed the old man sent Rufus riding hard towards the Channel. To his third son Henry he presented a huge sum of money, five thousand pounds of silver, which Henry set about counting there and then so as to make sure he had not been short-changed.

Before he breathed his last, William ordered his prisoners-of-war to be freed and gifts of money to be made to selected churches – his admission fee to heaven. But as his followers rode off to secure their property ahead of the conflict that they could sense coming between the two elder sons, his servants plundered his personal possessions. The final indignity came when the gases that had accumulated in the Conqueror's rotting, corpulent body exploded – it had been forced into a coffin that was too small for it.

Usually respected, often feared, William the Conqueror had never been loved, and William Rufus was to rule in his father's tradition. He got his name, William the Red, from his florid complexion, which the superstitious saw as symbolising blood and fire. Historians disagree as to whether his hair was ginger or flaxen yellow, but there is no doubt about his complexion – red, the witches' colour – and William played up to this by sneering openly at religion. Why should he pray to God, he once asked after suffering a severe illness, since God had caused him such pain and trouble? When senior churchmen – abbots and bishops – died, Rufus blocked the appointment of a successor, so he could take over their lands and keep the income for himself. It was scarcely surprising that the churchmen who wrote the history of the times should have given him a bad press. On the basis of their criticisms, William the Red has gone down in history as one of England's 'bad' kings.

In fact, he ruled England quite effectively, if harshly, in the Norman style. He defeated the attempts of his elder brother Robert Curthose to claim England, taking the battle to Robert in Normandy. In London William built ambitiously, constructing the first stone bridge over the River Thames, and a huge banqueting hall down the river in Edward the Confessor's Palace of Westminster.

Westminster Hall stands to this day, and is the most ancient section of the Houses of Parliament. The tall and echoing hall was the home of the law courts for centuries and, since 1910, the place where dead kings and queens lie in state. In April 2002 some two hundred thousand mourners queued for hours to file silently through William Rufus's nine-hundred-year-old banqueting hall to pay their last respects at the coffin of Queen Elizabeth the Queen Mother.

The Red King loved hunting. It was a passion with all the Norman monarchs, and a deep source of grievance to their English subjects. More than seventy forests around England were eventually to be designated royal hunting preserves where special forest laws were fiercely enforced by the King's foresters and 'wood-wards'. Anyone caught hunting deer, boar or other game there was punished with blinding or mutilation. You could be punished just for carrying a bow and arrow. People inside the royal forest areas, which included open fields and whole villages, were not allowed to keep dogs, unless the animal had been disabled from hunting by having three digits cut from one of its front paws. These are the years when rabbits and pheasants first appeared in England, introduced by the Normans to add to their hunting pleasures. But for Saxon farmers these new arrivals, like the royal deer, were simply crop-consuming pests.

The New Forest, south of Winchester, was the subject of a particular grievance. It was quite literally new, recently created by expelling people from their farms and villages, and William Rufus was hunting there on 2 August 1100 when a curious accident occurred. It was late in the afternoon, the sun was setting, and the King had to shade his eyes against the light. The royal hunting party was strung out at different stands in the forest, waiting for the rangers to chase up and drive the deer through the undergrowth across their line of fire. The King was with one of his favourite hunting companions, Walter Tyrel, a Norman nobleman who was an excellent shot. But somehow the usually accurate Tyrel missed his deer and fired directly into William's chest. Reaching to tear out the arrow, William succeeded only in breaking off the shaft, and as he fell to the ground the arrowhead was driven deeper into his chest.

It was what happened next that suggests that this shooting was no accident, for Tyrel rode straight out of the forest and headed for the coast, where he took a boat to France. He had left the King's body lying on the forest floor, where it was retrieved by local farm labourers and thrown on to a cart, to be trundled over the rutted lanes to Winchester. 'Blood dripped freely the whole way', according to William of Malmesbury, writing a few years later.

Tyrel's strange behaviour could be explained in terms of sheer panic. But panic was anything but the reaction of William's younger brother Henry, who was one of the royal hunting party that day. Henry had been at another stand in the forest with Tyrel's brothers-in-law, Gilbert and Roger of Clare. We do not know who brought Henry the news of his brother's death, but his reaction was as instant as Tyrel's. He rode straight to Winchester to secure the royal treasury, and was proclaimed king next day. He then rode on to London, where he was solemnly crowned in Westminster Abbey on 5 August – just three days after the death of his brother, who was buried with scant ceremony at Winchester.

The chroniclers had no doubt that the death of William Rufus was inspired by God himself, to punish a monarch who had derided and exploited the Church. At the time, Rufus was enjoying the income of no less than twelve abbeys that he had deliberately kept abbotless – 'without shepherds', as William of Malmesbury put it. No wonder God should strike down 'a soul who could not be saved'.

Today we might scan the evidence for a more earthly plotter. William's brother, Henry, now sat securely on the throne of England. Walter Tyrel was never investigated or punished for the slaying of William the Red; and it was curious that among those to whom the new king showed special favour were Walter Tyrel's brothers-in-law, Gilbert and Robert of Clare.

HENRY I AND
THE WHITE SHIP

AD 1120

TEN YEARS BEFORE HE BECAME KING, WILLIAM the Conqueror's youngest son Henry was helping to put down an uprising in the Norman city of Rouen. It was the late autumn of 1090, and after the fighting had ended he invited the leader of the rebellion to a high tower where he could look out over the walled city and admire the beautiful river and surrounding green fields and woods that he had been trying to conquer. Then he personally threw the man out of the window.

Henry I was thirty-two when he became King of England, and had shown himself to be both decisive and single-minded after the mysterious shooting of his brother Rufus. Now he set about capturing Normandy from his other brother, Robert Curthose. In 1106 he defeated Robert at the Battle of Tinchebrai, south of Bayeux – fought, by coincidence, on 28 September, the date on which William the Conqueror had landed his troops in Sussex in 1066. So forty years later to the day, William's youngest son had reunited his father's cross-Channel empire. Henry consigned his brother Robert to successive prisons at Wareham, Devizes, Bristol and finally Cardiff, where the unhappy Short-stockings would spend the last months of his twenty-eight-year imprisonment learning Welsh.

'Woe to him that is not old enough to die,' declared Robert Curthose, who finally expired in 1134 at the age of eighty, and whose tomb can be seen today in Gloucester Cathedral.

'Exchequer' is a modern word that comes to us from the reign of Henry I – a king with a sharp eye for a penny. We have seen him counting the silver his father gave him on his deathbed for his inheritance, then galloping straight to the treasury when his brother died; he was the last king for four hundred years shrewd enough to die without any debts. Now, sometime after 1106, he introduced the exchequer as a revolutionary new method of government accounting and of centralising royal power. Based on the Middle Eastern abacus or counting-frame, the exchequer was a chequered cloth like a chessboard. Counters were piled on the different squares, rather as croupiers handle chips on a gaming table. Twice a year, at Easter and Michaelmas (the feast of St Michael on 29 September), the sheriffs and royal officials from the shires had to bring their money to be checked and counted. To this day, the cabinet minister in charge of the nation's finances is known as the Chancellor of the Exchequer, and we all write and, if we are lucky, also sometimes cash 'cheques'.

By 1120 Henry I controlled a well-financed empire on the two sides of the English Channel. He travelled quite frequently from England to Normandy in his own longboat or *snecca*, a Norse word literally meaning 'snake' or 'serpent'. Merchants and nobles criss-crossed the channel on these medieval equivalents of the cross-Channel ferry, which, according to records from the next century, charged two pence for an ordinary passenger and twelve for a knight with his horse. In tapestries and paintings of the time the boats are depicted with striped sails, complete with masts, rigging, tillers and anchors. Often their prows were decorated with figureheads of dragons and other beasts.

As Henry was preparing to set sail from the Norman port of Barfleur at the end of November 1120, he was approached by a young seafarer, Thomas FitzStephen. Thomas's father, Stephen, had been William the Conqueror's personal sea captain, taking him on the historic voyage of 1066 to fight against Harold, and he had ferried him back and forth across the Channel to the end of his life. Now his son Thomas had a newly fitted-out snakeship of which he was particularly proud, the *White Ship*, and he offered it to the King for his voyage.

Henry had already made his travelling arrangements, but he suggested it would be a treat for his son and heir, William, to sail on this state-of-the-art vessel. William was just seventeen and a young man on whom many hopes rode. He was popularly nicknamed 'the Aetheling', the old Anglo-Saxon title meaning 'throne-worthy' (see p. 65), because his mother

Edith-Matilda was descended from King Alfred's royal house of Wessex. Here was a part-Saxon heir – some much-cherished English blood – who would one day inherit the Normans' empire.

Henry set sail for England, leaving William the Aetheling to follow in the *White Ship*, with many of the court's most lively young blades, among them William's half-brother Richard and his half-sister Matilda, two of the numerous illegitimate children that Henry had fathered outside his marriage to Edith-Matilda. Spirits were high as the *White Ship* loosed its moorings. Wine flowed freely among passengers and crew, and as darkness fell, the princely party issued a dare to the captain – that he should overtake the King's ship, which was already out at sea.

The *White Ship*'s fifty oarsmen heaved with all their might to pull clear of the harbour, but as the vessel made its way through the night its port side struck violently against a rock that lay hidden just below the surface of the water. This rock was a well-known hazard of the area, uncovered each day as the tide ebbed, then submerged at high tide. It can be seen to this day from the cliffs of Barfleur, a dark shadow lurking beneath the water. But Captain Thomas FitzStephen, like his passengers, had been drinking, and the ship's wooden hull shattered on the rock, the vessel capsizing almost immediately. It was still close enough to the shore for the cries and screams of its three hundred passengers and crew to be mistaken for drunken revelry. According to one account the passengers on the royal snakeship heard the cries behind them, but sailed on, unheeding, towards England, through the night.

The *White Ship* was the *Titanic* of the Middle Ages, a

much-vaunted high-tech vessel on its maiden voyage, wrecked against a foreseeable natural obstacle in the reckless pursuit of speed. The passenger list constituted the cream of high society, cast into the chilly waters. Orderic Vitalis, an Anglo-Norman chronicler of the time, described the scene:

> *The rays of the moon lit up the world for about nine hours, showing up everything in the sea to the mariners. Thomas, the skipper, gathered his strength after sinking for the first time and, remembering his duty, lifted his head as he came to the surface. Seeing the heads of the men who were clinging somehow to the spar, he asked, 'The king's son, what has become of him?' When the shipwrecked men replied that he had perished with all his companions, he said, 'It is vain for me to go on living.' With these words, in utter despair, he chose rather to sink on the spot than to die beneath the wrath of a king enraged by the loss of his son, or suffer long years of punishment in fetters.*

Orderic was wrong about the full moon. Sky tables show that on 25 November 1120 the moon was new, so the night must have been dark. But the chronicler does seem to have gathered his information, directly or indirectly, from the wreck's only survivor, a butcher from Rouen who had jumped on to the *White Ship* to collect some debts that were due to him from members of the court. The butcher was saved from the exposure that killed the others on that still, frosty night by the thick, air-retaining ram-skins he was wearing. Three fishermen plucked him out of the water next morning and took him back to dry land.

Over in England next day, King Henry became puzzled

when the *White Ship* did not dock or even appear on the horizon. But the news of the catastrophe reached the nobles at his court soon enough, and everyone discovered they had lost family and friends. Stewards, chamberlains and cup-bearers had all died – wives and husbands, sons and daughters. As the court mourned, no one dared break the dreadful news to the King, and a whole day and night went by before a young boy was finally pushed into the royal presence, weeping, to throw himself at the King's feet. When Henry realised what had happened, he fell to the ground himself, grief-stricken at the news. He had to be shepherded away to a room where he could mourn privately – this stern Norman king did not care to display weakness in public.

In the years following the death of his cherished son, King Henry I governed his realm as busily as ever, and also found time for his pleasures. He founded England's first zoo, where he kept lions and leopards, and a porcupine of which he was particularly fond. But he did confess to nightmares that terrified him so much that he would leap out of his bed and reach for his sword. He dreamed that his people – those who worked, those who fought, and those who prayed – were attacking him. The Conqueror's shrewd, harsh, penny-pinching youngest son had provided England and Normandy with firm government, but the wreck of the *White Ship* meant that Henry left no legitimate male heir to succeed him. The drowning of William the Aetheling was not just a personal tragedy – it would lead to England's first real and prolonged civil war.

STEPHEN AND MATILDA

AD 1135–54

KING HENRY I HAD A GREAT WEAKNESS FOR lampreys, small, eel-like creatures that sucked the blood of other fishes and were considered a delicacy in the Middle Ages. Worried at the havoc this oily parasite could wreak on the digestive system, Henry's doctor had banned the fish from the royal diet. But the King could not resist the temptation when his chefs served him up a plate of lampreys one late November evening in 1135 at the end of a day's hunting in the forest near Rouen in Normandy. The sixty-seven-year-old king was stricken with chills and convulsions on the Monday night, and by Sunday 1 December he was dead.

It was fifteen years since the tragic wreck of the *White Ship*, and Henry had not managed to solve the succession problem caused by the death of William the Aetheling, his only legitimate son. In 1127 he had got his barons to swear allegiance to his only other legitimate child, his daughter Matilda, then aged twenty-five, and, hoping to make doubly sure of their pledge, the old king had them repeat the exercise four years later. The unlikely prospect of a woman controlling the male-chauvinist barons of the Anglo-Norman realm might just have been feasible if Matilda had not been married to Geoffrey of Anjou, an ambitious young nobleman whom many Normans distrusted, and if Matilda herself had not been so heavy-handed. At the moment of Henry's death she had been quarrelling – not for the first time – with her father, and her absence from the deathbed cost her dear. The moment was seized by her nimble cousin Stephen of Blois, the son of Henry's sister Adela.

Controlling territory to the south of Normandy, the counts of Blois were powerful magnates with whom the Normans tried to stay on good terms. Stephen was an affable and well-liked character, popular with many of the Anglo-Norman barons. He was fortunate to have had a narrow escape in 1120 when he turned down an invitation to join the young hell-raisers on William the Aetheling's booze cruise. Stephen was then in his early twenties, and the chroniclers give two reasons why he decided not to board the *White Ship*: he disapproved of so much drinking, and he was suffering at the time from diarrhoea.

Maybe the diarrhoea had been an excuse, since it had not stopped him boarding the King's ship that night. Stephen was a quick-thinking man. The moment he realised in December 1135 that there was a crown for the taking, he followed the example of his uncles William Rufus and Henry himself and headed hell-for-leather for the royal treasury in Winchester. Three weeks later, England's first and last King Stephen was crowned in Westminster Abbey, just in time for Christmas.

But Matilda had her father's ferocious bloody-mindedness, and she was not willing to let her cousin steal her inheritance without a fight. The next twenty years would see Stephen and Matilda battling for control of England and Normandy, raising armies and bribing towns, bishops and barons to consolidate their cause. Matilda captured and imprisoned Stephen, then Stephen besieged her. In the winter of 1141, Matilda and her followers made a dramatic escape from Oxford Castle, dressed in white so they could not be seen against the snow. When Matilda held power, she alienated people with her overbearing ways. When Stephen had the whip hand he proved too soft and good-natured.

To start with, the barons saw themselves as the beneficiaries of this family rivalry, and they used the widespread unrest to settle old scores, often switching sides without a qualm. Loyalty hardly seemed to come into it. The *Anglo-Saxon Chronicle* described the situation in a famous passage on the woes of a land torn apart by civil war:

> *Every powerful man built himself castles and held them against the king . . . They sorely burdened the unhappy people of the country with forced labour, and when the castles were built, they*

filled them with devils and wicked men. By night and by day they seized those whom they believed had any wealth, ordinary men and women, and put them in prison to get their gold and silver and tortured them . . . They hung them up by their feet and smoked them with foul smoke. They hung them by the thumbs or by the head, then hung coats of mail [weighing about 25 kg] on their feet. They put knotted strings round their heads and twisted till it went to the brains. They put them in dungeons where there were adders and snakes and toads . . . Then when the wretched people had no more to give, they plundered and burned all the villages, so that you could easily go a day's journey without ever finding a village inhabited or field cultivated . . . Wherever the ground was tilled, the earth bore no corn, for the land was ruined by such doings. And men said openly that Christ and his saints slept.

Written by 1154, these vivid words come to us from Peterborough on the edge of the Fens, from the last monastery that was still producing editions of the *Anglo-Saxon Chronicle* – and which would itself stop the updatings at the end of Stephen's reign. The description quoted here was clearly based on the cruelty and destruction that the monks witnessed in their own neighbourhood; other parts of England may not have been so badly affected by what came to be known as the 'great anarchy'. But by the early 1150s, exhaustion had set in. The nobles were refusing to fight for either side, and there was a clear need for a settlement.

By then Matilda's cause was being fought by her forceful son, the red-headed Henry Plantagenet, so named after the bright-yellow broom flower known as the *planta genesta* that was the emblem of the counts of Anjou, his father's home territory to the south-west of Normandy. These Angevin rulers had a history of rivalry with the Normans, and Matilda's marriage to Geoffrey of Anjou had always hampered her cause. But Geoffrey died in 1151, and, having succeeded to the title, his son Henry married Eleanor of Aquitaine, whose vast territories to the south of Anjou included Gascony and the rich wine district of Bordeaux.

Henry Plantagenet was only twenty when he arrived in England in 1153, but through inheritance and marriage he controlled almost half of France, a wide swathe down the western, Atlantic coast, and he had the soldiers to match. That winter he struck a deal for the succession, allowing the old and weary Stephen to remain on the throne for the rest of his lifetime, which lasted, in the event, barely a year. In December 1154 Matilda's son became King Henry II, the first ruler of England's new Angevin and Plantagenet dynasty.

Matilda had never been able to enjoy her inheritance. The closest she had come to being queen was to be styled the 'Lady of the English' during one of her brief periods of power. But she was to outlive her rival Stephen by a dozen years, and she had the pleasure of seeing her son, the new king, reign over a vast empire that stretched from Hadrian's Wall to the Pyrenees.

MURDER IN THE CATHEDRAL

AD 1170

KING HENRY II AND HIS CHANCELLOR Thomas Becket were the closest of friends. People declared the two men 'had but one heart and one mind'. The new Plantagenet king was twenty-one when he came to the throne in 1154. Thomas Becket, a London merchant's son, was in his mid-thirties, but the difference in their ages and status did not seem to matter. They hunted and played chess together – and both were furious workers. Henry was consumed by the challenge of holding together his diverse and disorderly collection of territories in England and France. Thomas, appointed his chancellor at the start of the reign, was in charge of the royal writing office, drawing up official documents and firing off letters. One clerk later recalled that before taking dictation from Becket he would have to get at least sixty, and sometimes as many as a hundred, quill pens cut and sharpened in advance – he knew there would be no time for sharpening during the session.

Business from all over Henry's Angevin empire passed through Thomas's hands, and he revelled in the glory of his position. Imitating his master's grandfather, Henry I, Thomas kept exotic animals – monkeys, and a couple of wolves that he had trained for hunting their own kind, which still lurked in the royal forests. When he went to France in 1158 to negotiate a marriage treaty for one of Henry's daughters, he travelled in fabulous luxury.

'If this be only the Chancellor,' marvelled onlookers, 'what must be the glory of the King himself?'

Henry would tease Thomas wryly about his grandeur. As the two men rode together through London one winter's day, the King saw a poor man shivering in the cold and suggested that he needed a coat. Thomas agreed – whereupon Henry grabbed at his chancellor's magnificent fur-lined scarlet cloak, and the two friends wrestled together until Thomas gave way.

Henry II was proud of the law and order that he had brought to his so recently chaotic realm. He would refer contemptuously to the reign of his predecessor as the years of 'disorder', as if King Stephen had never been. It was in Henry's reign that the legal status of the jury, first introduced by the Danes, took firm root, and from this time comes the word 'assizes', from the Norman French for 'sitting'. The King's judges would travel from county to county, sitting in justice over the people to administer the common law – the law that applied to all free men.

The exception was the Church, which had its own courts and a law of its own. If a priest murdered or raped or stole, he could avoid the common-law penalties of hanging or mutilation by claiming 'benefit of clergy', the right to be tried in the bishop's court, which could do no worse than defrock him – expel him from the priesthood – and impose a penance. Common law stopped at the church door, and some clerics were major powers in the land. Rich bishops and abbots enjoyed the revenues of large estates, with their own retinues and sometimes mini-armies. Although they swore loyalty to the King, they insisted that their earthly oaths must rank below their loyalty to God and to his supreme earthly representative, the Pope in Rome.

When the Archbishop of Canterbury died in 1161, Henry saw the chance to tackle the problem. He would give the job to his best friend, who would use his energy and loyalty to put the Church in its place while at the same time remaining his chancellor. But Henry – along with almost everyone who had ever seen the two men together – was astonished when the new archbishop insisted on resigning his position as chancellor and almost immediately started to champion the rights of the Church. Becket publicly opposed Henry's attempts to levy a tax that applied to bishops as well as to barons, and when it came to the vexed question of Church versus common law, he took the position that priests should never be subject to the death penalty. With the donning of his archbishop's robes, the King's worldly comrade had become his pious and prickly opponent, dedicated to frustrating the very changes he had been put in place to implement.

What made Becket change? The elegant chancellor's

startling transformation has been debated ever since, not least by playwrights and poets from Alfred Lord Tennyson to T. S. Eliot, who have created stirring dramas from the change in character that turned dear friends into mortal enemies. Thomas had been 'born again', it seemed. From being the King's man, he became God's man – as he saw his God, at least. But there were those in the Church who suggested that the change had not been as total as it seemed. There had always been something artificial about the glittering Thomas, something of the actor. Becket could never resist catching the public eye: he loved being a celebrity. Gilded companion of the King or sackcloth servant of the Church, he never failed to act his part – or to overact it – superbly.

'An ass he always was,' remarked Gilbert Foliot, the Bishop of London, 'and an ass he'll always be.'

Foliot was a broad-minded churchman in the tolerant tradition of Bede. He understood the need for compromise between Church and state, and, like other senior clerics, he openly opposed the obstinacy of the new archbishop.

But compromise had never been a word in Thomas's vocabulary, and he now pursued God's cause in a succession of confrontations that came to a head in October 1164. Becket arrived at Northampton Castle to answer Henry's complaints, with a large retinue of clerks and monks and an armoured bodyguard. He insisted on carrying the massive silver cross of Canterbury in his own hands to signify that he was claiming God's protection against the King.

'Perjurer!' shouted the barons who supported Henry and felt that Thomas had broken his oath of loyalty to him. 'Traitor!'

Born-again Becket gave as good as he got, temporarily forsaking his saintly demeanour to retort 'Whoremonger!' at the baron who organised the King's mistresses, and 'Bastard!' at Henry's illegitimate brother. Anticipating arrest and captivity, Thomas then slipped out of the castle before dawn by an unguarded gate, and made his way in disguise to the south coast where he took a small boat to Flanders, and then on to France.

In the six years of exile that followed, Henry and Thomas met three times in France to try to patch up their differences – encounters that were fraught with emotion. In July 1170 in a field near the banks of the River Loire, Thomas was so overcome that he jumped off his horse and threw himself to the ground in front of Henry. The King responded by himself dismounting. Then he took hold of his old friend and forced him back into the saddle, holding his stirrup so as to help him up.

On this occasion the two men had been arguing over a crowning ceremony that Henry had arranged for his eldest son earlier that summer in an attempt to solidify the royal succession. In Thomas's absence, Henry had called in the Archbishop of York and Gilbert Foliot of London, with other bishops, to consecrate the ceremony. The crowning hijacked a job that archbishops of Canterbury had always jealously preserved as their own, but Becket agreed to return to England, all the same.

Back in Canterbury, however, and preaching from the cathedral pulpit on Christmas Day, the restored archbishop denounced the bishops who had taken part in the illegal crowning.

'May they all be damned by Jesus Christ!' he cried, hurling flaming candles to the floor.

Over in Normandy, Henry flew into a tantrum of his own. 'Will no man rid me of this turbulent priest?' is the cry that legend has attributed to the furious king.

In fact, these words come from many centuries later, and there is much better evidence from closer to the time. Within two years of the episode Edward Grim, a priest on Becket's staff who was personally involved in the drama, reported Henry railing even more bitterly. 'What miserable drones and traitors have I nourished and promoted in my household, who let their lord be treated with such shameful contempt by a lowborn cleric?'

Four of his knights took this cry as a summons to action. They crossed the Channel to Kent, stopping at Saltwood Castle to mobilise an arrest party, then rode on to Canterbury. When they arrived at the cathedral on 29 December 1170, the archbishop had just finished his lunch. It was around three in the afternoon when the visitors were ushered into his bedroom, and though they had taken off their sword-belts as a gesture of courtesy, Thomas studiously ignored them at first. He certainly knew at least three of the knights personally, but he chose to treat them with disdain, angrily rejecting their request that he should accompany them to Winchester.

A shouting match ensued. As tempers rose, the knights waved their arms about and twisted their heavy gloves into knots, according to one eyewitness. Their leader Reginald FitzUrse – literally Reginald 'Bear-son' – ordered the archbishop's followers to leave, and when they refused, led his own men out of the room to get their weapons. Thomas seemed almost disappointed that they were retreating.

'Do you think I'm going to sneak off?' he cried. 'I haven't returned to Canterbury in order to run away. You'll find me here. And in the Lord's battle, I'll fight hand to hand, toe to toe.'

'Why should you annoy them further,' remonstrated one of his followers, 'by getting up and following them to the door?'

'My mind is made up,' replied Thomas. 'I know exactly what I have to do.'

'Please God,' came the reply, 'that you have chosen well.'

By four o'clock Thomas was in the cathedral. It was getting dark. In the candlelit church, the monks were just finishing their devotions and townsfolk were arriving for public evensong. Meanwhile, the knights were out in the cloisters, pulling on their armour and strapping on their sword-belts.

'Where is the traitor?' they shouted as they broke into the cathedral. 'Where is the archbishop?'

'Here I am,' replied Becket. 'No traitor to the king, but a priest of God!'

We know these words and all the dramatic details of what happened next in the cathedral that fading December evening, because no less than four of Becket's followers recorded their own accounts of the tragedy – with first-hand vividness, and considerable honesty as well. One admitted that he ran off and hid behind the altar as soon as the fighting started. But Edward Grim was made of sterner stuff, and he stayed beside Becket as the knights moved in to lay hands on the archbishop. Becket, a strong man, robustly wrestled them off, and as Grim put up a hand to shield his master, a sword struck through his arm to the bone, then rebounded, flying onwards to slice into the top of Becket's head.

'He received a second blow on the head,' wrote Grim, 'but still stood firm. At the third blow he fell on his knees and elbows, offering himself a living victim and saying in a low voice, "For the name of Jesus and the protection of the church, I am ready to embrace death."'

Grim described the grisly details as a further blow cut Becket's skull right open, spilling 'blood white with the brain, and the brain red with the blood' on to the cathedral floor.

'Let's be off, knights!' cried one of the assassins. 'This fellow won't be up again!'

The eyewitness accounts make clear that in the initial terrible shock of such violence, few people saw the slaying as a martyrdom. It was Becket's own confrontational style that had turned the arrest party into murderers – and some even suggested that Becket had provoked the disaster through his own arrogance.

'He wanted to be a king – he wanted to be more than a king,' was one angry reaction. 'Let him be a king now!'

But then the monks started readying Thomas's body for burial, and as they cut away his bloodstained outer vestments, the surprising garment they discovered underneath changed their attitude entirely.

'Look,' cried one, 'he's a true monk!'

A KING REPENTS

AD 1174

I F THOMAS BECKET HAD BEEN WEARING SILK
underpants when he died, he might never have become a
martyr. Luxurious clothing would have confirmed all the
worst suspicions about his vainglorious pride. But as
Thomas's confused followers stripped off his bloodied vestments on the evening of 29 December 1170 to prepare his
body for burial, they discovered the very opposite of luxury.
Next to the skin of the murdered archbishop was a shirt of
the roughest goat's hair, extending from his neck to his
knees. It was the ultimate monkish symbol of humility, the
painfully itchy garment that the pious wore when they
wished to punish themselves – and Thomas had taken

self-punishment to extremes. His hair shirt was crawling with maggots and lice.

This was the moment when the process of sainthood began. The discovery of the hair shirt, we are told, astonished everyone except Thomas's private chaplain Robert of Merton, the archbishop's spiritual confidant, who had been in charge of his private devotions. These included, it now turned out, the trussing-up of the heavy hair shirt as many as three times a day, so the chaplain could whip the archbishop's back until the blood flowed – and if the man tired, Thomas would tear at his flesh with his own fingernails.

We might well say today that such appalling masochism was reason in itself for Thomas's incurably prickly attitude towards the world. But in Canterbury Cathedral that evening in 1170 the monks knew they had been confronted with proof of the dead archbishop's saintliness. Thomas had mortified his body in order to master his carnal desires. Otherworldly in this last stage of his life, Becket had moved to the ultimate dimension in the manner and place of his dying, and the monks promptly set about collecting his blood in a basin. The martyr was decked out for burial in the cathedral crypt, wearing his hair shirt below his glorious robes, and carrying his ceremonial shepherd's staff of office.

All Europe was shocked by the murder in the cathedral. The tale reached as far as Iceland, where it became the 'Thómas Saga', and in the scandalised retellings the complexity of Becket's love–hate relationship with his former friend became simplified. Henry Plantagenet was cast as the villain. The Pope declared Thomas a saint, and ordered the King to do penance.

In the summer of 1174, dressed for the occasion in a hair shirt of his own, Henry went humbly to Canterbury, where he spent a day and a night fasting on the bare ground beside Thomas's tomb. Around him lay ordinary pilgrims, so the news of the royal humiliation would be publicly known and spread. The King offered himself for five strokes of the rod from every bishop present, and three from each of Canterbury's eighty monks. Then, wearing around his neck a phial of water that had been tinctured with drops of Becket's blood, Henry dragged himself on to his horse and rode back to London, where he took to his bed.

'Canterbury Water' became a must-buy for the countless pilgrims who flocked to Becket's tomb in the centuries that followed. The precious pink liquid was said to heal the blind and raise the crippled, and the streets around the cathedral became crammed with souvenir stalls selling badges and highly coloured images of the martyr. The tomb itself was a stupendous sight, sparkling with jewels and hung about with the sticks and crutches of those whom the visit had revivified – a gaudy spectacle of salvation. From relative obscurity, Canterbury became one of Europe's premier religious destinations, ranking with Rome, Jerusalem, Santiago de Compostela and the continent's other great centres of pilgrimage.

England took pride in its home-grown hero who so enhanced the country's spiritual status in Christendom, and no one embraced the devotion of Thomas more enthusiastically than the royal family. Henry II's three daughters, married to the rulers of Sicily, Saxony and the Spanish kingdom of Castile, spread the cult of the English saint with chapels, lavish wallpaintings and mosaics. The obstinate individual

who had dared to defy their father was no longer a villain –
he was an icon of English identity – and in later centuries
even the name of this London merchant's son became
fancified. He came to be known as Thomas 'à' Becket.

The prestigious new cult and enhanced tourist business
were some consolation for the fact that Henry had lost his
great battle with the Church. It had been a major defeat. In
addition to his public penance, the King had to agree that
England's church courts should remain independent of the
common law. Priests continued to enjoy the 'benefit of
clergy' for centuries, and from a modern perspective clerical
privilege might not seem a worthy cause for which to die.
But the archbishop had spoken his mind. He had stood up
to authority he considered unjust and he had been prepared
to lay down his life for his beliefs. Goat-hair shirt or silk
underpants – either way, Thomas Becket had walked the
path of the hero.

THE RIVER-BANK TAKE-AWAY

AD 1172

IN 1172 WILLIAM FITZSTEPHEN, ONE OF THE
eyewitnesses at the death of Thomas Becket, described
what you would see if you visited the bustling city of London
in the reign of England's first Plantagenet king:

> On the east stands the Tower, exceeding great and strong, whose
> walls and bailey rise from very deep foundations, their mortar
> being mixed with the blood of beasts. On the west are two strongly
> fortified castles, while from them there runs a great continuous
> wall, very high, with seven double gates, and towers at intervals
> along its north side. On the south, London once had similar
> walls and towers. But the Thames, that mighty river teeming with

fish, which runs on that side and ebbs and flows with the sea, has in the passage of time washed those bulwarks away, undermining them and bringing them down ... On all sides, beyond the houses, lie the gardens of the citizens that live in the suburbs, planted with trees, spacious and fair, laid out beside each other. To the north are pasturelands and pleasant open spaces of level meadow, intersected by running waters, which turn millwheels with a cheerful sound.

FitzStephen wrote this description as a prologue to his life of Becket. He wanted to explain the background from which his hero had sprung and, as a fellow Londoner, he was clearly proud of England's largest city, which he praised for its Christian faith, for the wholesomeness of its air – and for its ability to enjoy itself.

At Easter, they make sport with tournaments on the river. A shield is firmly tied to a stout pole in midstream and a small boat, rowed with the current by many oarsmen, carries a young man standing in the bows, who has to strike the shield with his lance. His object is to break the lance by striking the shield and keeping his footing. But if he strikes it and does not splinter the lance, he falls into the river, and the boat goes on without him.

When the great marsh along the northern walls of the city is frozen, crowds of young men go out to amuse themselves on the ice. Some run to gather speed, and slide along the ice with feet apart covering great distances. Others make seats of ice shaped like millstones, and get a group of others who run in front of them, holding hands to drag them along. Sometimes they go too fast, and all fall flat on their faces. Others more skilled in ice sports fit the shin-bones of beasts to their feet, lashing them to their ankles, and use an iron-shod pole to propel themselves, pushing against the ice. They are borne along as swiftly as a bird in flight.

If England had had a tourist board in the twelfth century William FitzStephen would surely have been employed to write its brochures. A man of strong opinions, he contended that the men of London were famous for their honour and the women for their chastity. He produced no evidence to back up these claims, but he did describe a city with at least one facility that sounds both modern and convenient:

Moreover there is in London on the river-bank, amid the wine sold from ships and wine cellars, a public cook-shop. There daily you can find the seasonal foods, dishes roast, fried and boiled, fish of every size, coarse meat for the poor and delicate for the rich, such as venison and various kinds of birds. If travel-weary friends should suddenly call on any of the citizens, and do not wish to wait until fresh food is bought and cooked and 'till servants bring water for hands and bread', they hasten to the river-bank, where everything that they could want is ready and waiting . . . Those who desire to fare delicately need not search to find sturgeon or guinea-fowl . . . since every sort of delicacy is set out for them here.

RICHARD THE LIONHEART

AD 1189-99

JUST ONE ENGLISH KING HAS BEEN ACCORDED the honour of a statue outside the Houses of Parliament – Richard Coeur de Lion, the Lionheart, who sits magnificently on horseback, larger than life, wearing chain mail and brandishing his great sword over the car park between the Commons and the Lords. Richard is England's muscular hero king – our only ruler to have been captured and flung into a foreign dungeon – and it is not surprising that he has generated some fairytales. While in jail, according to one medieval legend, he had a love affair with the daughter of the German king who had captured him – to the fury of her father, who decided to stage an 'accident'. He gave orders for a lion in his private zoo to be starved for a few days, then to be allowed to 'escape' into Richard's cell. Hearing of the plan, the distraught princess begged her lover to flee, but Richard asked her instead for forty silk handker-chiefs. These he bound around his right forearm, and thus protected, when the beast broke into his cell, he thrust his arm down the lion's throat. Reaching inside its chest to tear out the heart, Richard strode to the Great Hall and flung it, still beating, on to the table in front of the astonished king. He then proceeded to sprinkle salt over the pulsating flesh and ate it with great relish – the Lionheart in deed and name.

Two years before he succeeded his father Henry II in 1189, Richard had sworn to 'take the Cross' – that is, to go on cru-sade – and his crusading oath defined almost everything about him. For a hundred years, Christian Europe had been consumed by the compulsion to clear Palestine of the Muslims, who controlled access to Jerusalem, Bethlehem and the other sites sacred to Christians in the Holy Land. The crusaders believed they possessed the one and only true faith, and that they were fighting in a just cause when they destroyed non-Christians. If they risked their lives in battle they increased their chances of going to heaven – a crusade was a pilgrimage with bloodshed added. Throw in a dash of vengeance and a call to liberation involving a simply identi-fied but distant place: here were the eternal constituents for self-righteous homicide.

At the moment when Christianity was securing its great-est ever hold over the hearts and minds of Europe – its mastery carved into the stone of the continent's great cathe-drals – non-believers were being seen by ordinary Christians as deeply threatening. Richard's accession was marked by England's first violent persecution of a minority group in the name of religion, when the Jews living in London and a number of other towns were attacked. The Jews had come to England with the Normans. They were a means by which the Normans financed their warfare, and they provided banking services to the rest of the community. They lent money on which they charged interest to merchants, landowners and also to the Church – many of England's great cathedrals and monasteries were built with money lent by the Jews.

But dependency provoked resentment among those who had borrowed, and they seized on the foreigners' unfamiliar costume, diet and other non-Christian practices as an alibi for taking revenge. Killing the lender was also a simple way of removing the debt. At Lynn in Norfolk and Stamford in Lincolnshire it was members of the local establishment – gentry and knights – who led the plundering of Jewish property. In York many of the several-hundred-strong Jewish community barricaded themselves inside the castle tower, whereupon they were besieged not only by rioters but by the sheriff's men who were supposed to protect them. Fearing their wives and children would be raped and mutilated, they killed them, then set fire to the tower and killed themselves.

To his credit, Richard tried personally to stop the anti-Semitic atrocities and made sure that the perpetrators of the York attack were punished. But when he arrived in Palestine on his crusade the following year, he showed no mercy to the Muslim infidels that he encountered.

In June 1191 he landed with his army at the port of Acre, which crusaders from several European countries had been besieging to no avail. Immediately, his powerful personality and his well organised forces gave him effective command of the attack. The city surrendered within five weeks. It was one of the great and rare triumphs in the two-hundred-year history of European crusading, establishing Richard as a solid-gold hero throughout Christendom. But when he felt that the Arabs were being slow in implementing the surrender agreement, he had no hesitation in parading 2700 hostages in front of the city and then having them slaughtered.

It is the folk-memory of such killings that has led Osama bin Laden and Arab leaders such as Saddam Hussein and Muammar Gaddafi to describe modern Western invaders of the Middle East, particularly Britain and America, as 'crusaders'. They see a direct connection, and they view the modern state of Israel, sponsored and so heavily supported by America, as the West's revenge for the failure of its crusades. In the Middle Ages the Arab inhabitants of Palestine generally extended more tolerance to Christians – and to the small number of Jews then living there – than the Christians were prepared to show to them. Saladin, the Kurdish leader of the Muslim forces, was conspicuous for his gallantry, entertaining enemy leaders with courtesy and generosity – though his soldiers, like the crusader armies, were ultimately held together by religious fanaticism. Muslims who died in this jihad, or holy war, were promised instant entry to heaven.

In his sixteen months of campaigning, Richard failed to capture his main goal, Jerusalem. But he did secure Acre and a strip of territory that provided a toehold for Christian influence. And when it came to hand-to-hand combat, he proved himself a royal Rambo: 'With no armour on his legs, he threw himself into the sea first . . . and forced his way powerfully on to dry land', according to one account of how the Lionheart relieved the town of Jaffa in August 1192, showing no mercy to his opponents. 'The outstanding king shot them down indiscriminately with a crossbow he was carrying in his hand, and his elite companions pursued [them] as they fled across the beach, cutting them down'.

Richard's fame as a warrior owed as much to his organisational skills as to his bravery. Thanks to the care he took with the logistics, the English were the best-supplied, fed and watered of all the crusader armies. Before he left London, the King had arranged the manufacture and delivery of sixty thousand horseshoes – most from the iron forges of the Forest of Dean – along with fourteen thousand cured pig carcasses from Lincolnshire, Essex and Hampshire. He seldom let sentiment obstruct practicality. In England he had been presented with an ancient and mighty sword found in Glastonbury and said to be King Arthur's Excalibur. But when he reached Sicily Richard exchanged the mythical weapon for four supply ships. The Lionheart was so busy creating his own legend he had no need of anyone else's.

It was on his way back from the Holy Land that he inspired the most memorable legends of all. Hugging the shore in an attempt to avoid the winter storms of the open Mediterranean, he was shipwrecked in December 1192 on the northern Adriatic coast (now Slovenia), and travelling north towards home he entered the territory of the Austrian duke Leopold with whom he had quarrelled during the siege of Acre. The English king and his companions tried to disguise themselves in hoods and cloaks as returning pilgrims, but they were captured and flung into the dungeons of Castle Durnstein, high on a crag above the River Danube.

Richard did not spend long behind bars. As Christendom's most famous warrior, he was a high-profile bargaining chip to be paraded by Leopold and the German emperor – the king in the fairytale of the forty handkerchiefs. But it was over a year before England came up with the 100,000 silver crowns – the equivalent of three years' taxation – required to ransom its walkabout king, and from this captivity came both the legend of the hungry lion and the story of Blondel the royal minstrel.

Richard was music-mad. He loved to conduct the choir in his chapel, and he composed ballads in the style of the courtly troubadours of Aquitaine, where he grew up and which he always considered his home. According to the legend, he had composed a ballad to a lady of the court with the help of Blondel, a ministrel who was devoted to him. The moment Blondel heard of his master's captivity, he set off for Germany, singing the first line of the ballad outside every castle he passed, until finally he reached Castle Durnstein. There he heard, wafting through the bars of the dungeon, the melodious voice that told him that Richard was alive and well.

Like the tale of the silk handkerchiefs and the lion's heart, this story sprang up within a few decades of Richard's death. When people later recalled the imprisonment of their crusader king they opted for fantasy, forgetting the unprecedented expense that his ransom had imposed on England. The ransom tax swelled the considerable sums already shelled out by those back home to finance his crusade, and it was followed by even heavier taxes to sustain the battles that Richard started fighting in France as soon as he got back to Europe. But as we smile, perhaps patronisingly, at the thought of these poor put-upon medievals, let us reflect on the disposal of our taxes today. In the spring of 2003 Tony Blair promised he would spend 'whatever it takes' to support the British troops fighting in Iraq, and, despite people's doubts about the war, the opinion polls showed broad agreement with that particular use of taxpayers' money. Who would dare to put a price on patriotism?

The abandonment of reason that national feeling can provoke seems the likeliest explanation of England's fondness down the years for the warlike Lionheart – a character venerated enough to be played on the screen by Sir Sean Connery. In reality, England's hero king did not speak English. His native language was French, and he saw himself as an Angevin, building up the French empire of his father Henry and his mother, Eleanor of Aquitaine. As he lay dying in 1199, aged only forty-one, following a crossbow wound he had received during the siege of the French castle of Chalus, Richard arranged that his body, disembowelled and salted, should be sent for burial beside his parents at the abbey of Fontevrault in Anjou. As a final touch, he instructed that his famous Coeur de Lion – which turned out to be 'of great size' – be cut out and sent, not to England, but to Normandy.

Yet Richard did bequeath to England an enduring emblem of the martial qualities he embodied. As the English crusaders fought in the Holy Land they often heard the French soldiers cry out to their patron saint, St Denys, and they decided they would like a patron of their own. There was a whole gallery of English martyrs they could have invoked, from St Alban to the recently canonised St Thomas of Canterbury. But none of these was warlike enough, and so they lighted on a local campaigner. St George was a Christian martyr, thought to be of Turkish or Arab descent, who had died at Lydda in Palestine around AD 303. Many centuries later, the legend that he slew a dragon to save a damsel in distress was attached to his name, together with the symbol of a striking red cross on a plain white field – and the tale evidently caught Richard's fancy. The King placed himself and his army in the Holy Land under George's protection.

It was several hundred years before St George became fully established as England's patron saint, and he has never been exclusively ours. Portugal regards him as its patron, as do the great Italian seaport cities of Venice and Genoa. But Richard spread himself pretty thin as well. In the course of his ten-year reign he spent just six months in England. So a king who was not English helped supply us with the saint who was not English – hybrid symbols for a mongrel race.

JOHN LACKLAND AND
MAGNA CARTA

AD 1215

BEFORE HE DIED, HENRY II, THE FATHER OF Richard the Lionheart, commissioned a painting that showed an eagle being pecked to death by its young.

'Those are my sons,' Henry would say.

The painting hung in his palace at Winchester, and showed one of the eaglets poised on its father's neck, waiting for the moment to peck out its eyes. That particularly vicious nestling was John, explained the old king – 'the youngest of them, whom I now embrace with so much affection' – and he predicted that his favourite son would one day betray him.

So it proved. Henry had four adult sons (two of whom, Henry the Younger and Geoffrey, would predecease their father), and he worried that the youngest had no inheritance. He nicknamed the boy 'Jean sans Terre' – John Lackland – and the fond father provoked a series of bitter family battles by trying to pare off bits of the other brothers' inheritances to give to John. In the Middle Ages a royal family battle could be just that. In 1189 the furious Richard led an army against his ailing father so as to compel him to hand over his birthright. As he marched across France his forces were swelled by many who calculated that the old man had become a lost cause and that they had nothing to lose by rallying to the Lionheart.

'Woe, woe,' Henry muttered, 'on a vanquished king!'

Just a few days from death, Henry II was compelled to surrender, asking only that he be told the names of those who had switched sides to support Richard. The old man was shown the list – and John's name was at the head of it.

Having betrayed one member of the family, John then set about betraying another. If Richard is the Prince Charming of English history, John is the pantomime villain. No sooner had Richard left on crusade for the Holy Land in 1189, than John started plotting to steal England from him. When the news came through of Richard's capture and imprisonment in Germany, he conspired with King Philip II of France to keep Richard in jail.

'Look to yourself,' Philip warned John when he discovered their plot had failed, 'the devil is loosed!'

It was a measure of the Lionheart's chivalry that he forgave his younger brother when he arrived back in England and John pleaded for mercy.

'Think no more of it, John,' he said. 'You are only a child' –

and the King took the twenty-seven-year-old child off for a feast of freshly caught salmon.

John succeeded Richard in 1199 when the Lionheart died without legitimate offspring, and for most people their experience of the new reign was no different from the old. Nobles, townspeople, farmers – all were taxed and taxed again as John went about campaigning in an effort to hold together the extensive family lands in France. But while Richard's military adventures had yielded romantic glory, John had little to show but defeat. *Mollegladium* (Softsword) became his Latin nickname according to the monkish chroniclers, who paint a disapproving picture of an idle and luxury-loving king, gloating over his jewels and spending long hours in bed.

As churchmen they were biased witnesses, since much of John's reign was dominated by long-running conflict with the Church. In 1205 a dispute arose over the election of a new Archbishop of Canterbury, and John refused to accept the Pope's candidate. His Holiness responded with an interdiction on the whole of England – a general 'lock-out' by the clergy. Churches were closed, the bells tied up and silenced. For six years the clergy held no services in church, refusing to perform baptisms, weddings or funerals. You might get the priest to come to your home privately to bless your baby or your son's marriage, and masses with sermons were still held once a week. But these had to take place outside the shuttered churches, in the often damp and chilly churchyard. The priest might also attend deathbeds to administer the last sacraments, but after that the people had to bury their loved ones in ditches or woodlands, making do with their own improvised prayers.

If religion is the opium of the people, Britain went without its fix for six years. People were in fear for their immortal souls. Without being fully welcomed into the Church, they believed, their children could be possessed by devils; without proper burial they might not get to heaven. For a faith-based society, the years of the interdiction were a grievous and demoralising time. In the Holy Land the English had recently been numbered among God's heroes. Now they were cast out among the goats.

In 1209 John was singled out personally by the Pope for excommunication – a total rejection by the Church, even worse than interdiction, and a badge of shame that condemned him to hellfire and damnation. Every bishop but one left the country, and in the end John caved in. He accepted the Pope's candidate as Archbishop of Canterbury and the interdiction was lifted in mid-1214. But when England suffered military disaster that summer, the humiliation could not help seeming like the judgement of God. John had already lost control of Normandy to the King of France, and the French victory at Bouvines on 27 July 1214 made the loss final.

Softsword had something of the snake about him. It was not unusual for a medieval king simply to eliminate rivals, as John had done early in his reign when he imprisoned the son of his late brother Geoffrey – Arthur, who was never to be seen again. But when John later heard that a noblewoman had been gossiping about Arthur's disappearance, he had the culprit jailed with one of her sons and left them both to starve to death. The King gave the impression that he did not know how to play fair, that he would not hesitate to ride roughshod over anyone who crossed him. This, combined with his military failure, the church interdiction and his unrelenting tax demands, set the stage for the momentous and historic events of 1215.

In January of that year, a group of disgruntled barons who had gathered for the Christmas court called for the restoration of their 'ancient and accustomed liberties'. They seem to have been thinking of the sort of contract promising better behaviour on the part of the monarch that Ethelred the Unready had struck with his nobles and bishops in 1014. These ideas had been repeated by William the Conqueror's two sons, William Rufus and Henry I, when, in 1087 and 1100 respectively, they were canvassing for support after their throne-grabbing gallops to Winchester. It was Henry's coronation charter that now provided John's critics with a model.

In the spring of 1215 the barons decided to act. Assembling at Stamford in Lincolnshire, they started marching south, gathering support along the way. On 17 May sympathisers welcomed them to London, and their occupation of the city seems to have persuaded John to come to terms. After some preliminary discussions, the two sides met in the middle of June to negotiate on the banks of the Thames near Windsor in a meadow named Runnymede – literally, the 'soggy meadow' – and the result of several days' hard bargaining was the famous Magna Carta and a rather optimistic declaration of peace.

History has romanticised the Great Charter as the far-reaching document that established the people's liberties, when in many respects its purpose was scarcely grander than to protect the rights of the rich warrior landowners who were fed up with being so heavily taxed. The barons were certainly not fighting for the rights of the often downtrodden labourers, the serfs and villeins who worked on their estates ('serf' from the Latin word *servus* – 'slave' or 'servant'; 'villein' from *villa* – the country house that owned them). But, willy-nilly, the rights for which the barons fought had a universal application.

'No free man shall be seized, imprisoned, dispossessed, outlawed, exiled or ruined in any way . . .' read clause 39, 'except by the lawful judgement of his peers and the law of the land.' Here was a call for fair play and justice that would resonate in later years – and the following clause backed it up: 'To no one will we sell, to no one will we deny or delay right or justice.'

Other clauses regulated feudal landholding and inheritance, guaranteed towns their freedoms, and gave merchants the right of free travel. A start was made on reforming the hated laws that protected the royal hunting forests (see pp. 112-13), and a serious attempt was made to check abuses of power by local officials. Clause 35 set up the first country-wide system of standardised weights and measures – a bonus to trade and to all consumers.

All through the last days of June 1215, the clerks at Runnymede scribbled away furiously, making copies of the charter to be taken and read out in every shire of the land. Magna Carta was the first written document limiting the powers of the king to be backed up by practical enforcement. A watchdog council of twenty-five barons was set up to make sure the king obeyed the charter, and a commission of twelve knights in each county was charged to look into local abuses of the law.

It was the watchdog council that proved the snag. John refused to accept that a non-royal body should infringe his sacred power, while several of the twenty-five barons started to throw their new-found weight around. By the autumn, England was engulfed in civil war. The following spring Philip II of France sent an army under his son Louis to help the barons – if the English could invade France, why not vice versa? – and John spent the last months of his reign tramping the country in a vain attempt to quell the rebellion.

The final scene was staged that October in the misty wet-lands of East Anglia, where the royal baggage train struggled to cross the four-and-a-half-mile estuary of the Nene River (then known as the Wellstream) near Wisbech on the Wash. Misjudging the tide, the King's horses, wagons and riders were caught by the incoming waters. Jewels, gold and silver goblets, flagons, candelabra – even John's crown and corona-tion regalia – all were swallowed up by the sucking eddies of the Wash. The lost jewels of King John remain undiscovered treasure trove to this day.

The King himself was already sick with dysentery. After weeks of camp-fire food, he had overeaten when entertained by the townsfolk of Lynn and, according to one chronicler, his idea of a cure was to consume quantities of peaches and fresh-brewed cider. It was one delicacy too many. Borne to the nearby town of Newark on a stretcher of branches cut from Fen willows, John Lackland breathed his last on 18 October 1216.

Furious over the indignities of the interdiction, caused by John's refusal to do his Christian duty as they saw it, the monkish chroniclers of the time had no doubt which way his soul was headed. Hell was a foul place, wrote one, but it would now be rendered still more foul by the presence of King John. Disapproving of such moralistic judgements, 'value-free' modern historians have pointed to the growth of royal record-keeping during John's reign as evidence of how efficient his government administration was – as if bureaucratic efficiency was not one of our own modern gods.

But John's painstaking record-keeping has certainly provided us with some interesting insights into his life. The detailed inventory of what he lost in the watery East Anglian wastes included pieces of glass, which seem to have been portable windowpanes ready to be cut and fitted into the castles he visited. John was clearly a man who loved his comforts. We read in his accounts of William his bathman, paid a halfpenny a day for his services, with a few extra pence as a tip when he actually prepared a bath. The record shows us that John was unusually clean for his time – he took a bath every three weeks – while an entry describing 'an over-tunic for when his Lordship the King gets up in the night' reveals a further claim to distinction. John was England's first king to be recorded as owning a dressing-gown.

HOBBEHOD, PRINCE OF THIEVES

AD 1225

WHEN THE ROYAL JUDGES ARRIVED IN York in the summer of 1225, they found that one of the cases before them involved a certain Robert Hod (or Hood), an outlaw. Hod had failed to appear in court, so the judges duly confiscated his worldly goods, valued at the sum of thirty-two shillings and sixpence, which was about what it cost in the thirteenth century to live modestly for a year. Hod, or Hood, continued to steer clear of the justice system, for his penalty remained unpaid, and it was carried forward to the ledger for the following year under the name of 'Hobbehod' – which could mean 'that devil Hood', or might have been a spelling mistake for 'RobbeHod'.

That is the extent of the historical evidence we have for the possible existence of Robin Hood, the dashing outlaw of Sherwood Forest. But court records from Berkshire in 1261 tell us of another outlaw, this one described as 'William Robehod', and in the years that follow the Robehods or Robynhods proliferate in the records. Whether or not this particular bandit actually existed, his exploits were so famous that 'Robin Hood' became the medieval nickname for a fugitive from justice. Some outlaws chose it; others had it thrust upon them. By around 1400 a priest was complaining that people would rather hear 'a tale or a song of Robyn Hood' than listen to a sermon.

Robin and his Merrie Men have proved to have a timeless appeal, but in their own day they had a specific significance. You were proclaimed an outlaw if you repeatedly failed to show up at court to answer a charge. As with Hobbehod, a fugitive from the judges in 1225, your goods and chattels and any land you held were confiscated, and you would then have to take your chances outside the law. If you were captured, your death by hanging would be ordered without further trial, and if you resisted arrest anyone was entitled to kill you. To be a legally proclaimed fugitive was a perilous state of affairs, so no wonder that people's imaginations were captured by the dream of life under the greenwood tree, where you could live according to your own laws. It was a particularly satisfying option if the forest was one of those preserved for the king's hunting.

There had been legends about heroic brigands, bandits, and resistance fighters before Robin Hood, notably the stories surrounding Hereward, the Saxon nobleman deprived of his lands by the Normans. But Robin came a step or two down the social ladder from Hereward. The tales of the time described Hood as a 'yeoman', from the Danish word *yongerman*, a free peasant of the artisan class. He was a 'yeoman of the forest', spending his days in harmony with nature. And if the primitive philosophy of this 'good life' did not quite make Hobbehod a working-class hero, it could fairly be claimed that he was the original 'green' warrior.

Today you can visit the huge hollow oak tree in Sherwood Forest where Robin Hood and his band are supposed to have hidden from the wicked Sheriff of Nottingham. Sadly, the tree was not even an acorn at the end of the twelfth century, when legend claims the outlaw roamed the forest. King Richard was certainly in Nottingham in March 1194. He made a beeline for the town when he returned from imprisonment after the Crusades, for Nottingham had supported Prince John's attempts to supplant him, and its castle was the last to hold out for John's cause.

Richard instantly set up gallows in front of the castle walls, and proceeded to hang several soldiers, whose resistance may be attributed to their not knowing, or their refusal to believe, that the King was finally back.

'Well, what can you see?' asked Richard when at last the defenders sent envoys to negotiate. 'Am I here?'

The garrison promptly surrendered, and the King went off to celebrate with a day's hunting in Sherwood Forest. But there is no record of him ever meeting Robin Hood – and he cannot possibly have met Little John, Friar Tuck, Will Scarlet, Much the Miller's son, or any other of the subsequently named Merrie Men. Maid Marion would not appear in the proliferating network of Robyn Hood ballads, masques, and morris dances until the beginning of the sixteenth century, when she was often played for laughs by a male impersonator – an early example of the pantomime dame. It was around this period, three hundred years after Hobbehod's first non-appearance in court, that the national anti-hero's penchant for relieving passers-by of their spare cash was finally given a serious social purpose. In all his early portrayals Robin was a sturdy rascal – jovial, maybe, but basically a robber. Not until 1589 do we first read the claim that his followers 'tooke from rich to give the poore'.

So that devil Hood finally became England's symbol of resistance to tyranny, the archer of the green wood, daredevil justice maker, with his own programme of wealth redistribution in the days before the welfare state. Those are the noble and romantic aspects of the legend. But it is surely ironic that the national heart has been so stirred down the centuries by a man who started out a thief.

SIMON DE MONTFORT AND
HIS TALKING-PLACE

AD 1265

MAGNA CARTA DID NOT VANISH INTO THE
Wash with the rest of King John's baggage in October
1216. On the contrary, his death revived the Great Charter –
along with the fortunes of the monarchy. John's heir was
his nine-year-old son Henry, and the prospect of this child
being in charge of England somehow purged the bitterness
between Crown and barons. The country's quarrel had been
with John, and few people had welcomed the French army
that had come to the aid of the rebels. It is often said that no
foreign army has set foot on English soil since 1066, but
from May 1216 French troops were tramping over much of
south-east England, and during John's last desperate months

Louis, the son of the French king, was holding court in London.

To win over domestic opinion and help get rid of the French, who finally departed in September 1217, the young Henry III's guardians rapidly reissued the Great Charter – in modified form. They reworded or deleted a number of clauses, removing the controversial watchdog council of twenty-five barons that had sparked the civil war, but promised that the new king would rule according to the remaining provisions. When the boy king presided over a council meeting at Westminster the following year the charter was issued again, then affirmed for a third time in 1225 when Henry, by then seventeen, had been declared old enough to play a formal role in government. So, triply restated and confirmed, the idea of a contract between king and subjects became once more the basis of rule and law. When lawyers started collating English law in later centuries they listed the 1225 version of Magna Carta as the first in the Statute Book.

The trouble was that the new king himself had not the slightest intention of being accountable. A regulation-bound monarchy was not for Henry III. Humiliated by what he knew of his father's unhappy end, a fugitive in his own country skulking around the Fens, the latest Plantagenet was dedicated to the vision of glorious and absolute kingship. As he saw it, he was a ruler consecrated by God, with enough divinity in his fingertips to cure the sick with his touch.

The keynote project of Henry's reign was the rebuilding of Edward the Confessor's Westminster Abbey, which he demolished and had redesigned in the new, soaring gothic style – a temple to the historic past and, he hoped, to the magnificent future of England's kings. Henry installed the Confessor as the patron saint of this triumphal cult of royalty, reburying his remains in a shrine behind the high altar, the centrepiece of the new abbey. Henry even had a mural of Edward painted in his bedroom, so his saintly hero was the last thing he saw before he went to bed and the face that he woke up to in the morning.

Gazing up at the vaulted arches of Westminster Abbey, one can see that Henry III had a fine taste in architecture. But his judgement was poor when it came to just about everything else. A court jester is said to have remarked that, like Jesus Christ himself, Henry was as wise on the day of his birth as he would ever be. The contemporary chronicler Matthew Paris described him as 'of medium stature and compact in body. One of his eyelids drooped, hiding some of the dark part of the eyeball. He had robust strength, but was careless in his acts.'

In the eyes of England's barons, Henry was particularly careless in the choice of advisers and favourites, who, like his wife Eleanor of Provence, were almost all from southern France. In previous reigns, French dominance at court had reflected the powerbase of William the Conqueror. But King John had lost Normandy, Anjou and all of Aquitaine except for Gascony, the wine region around Bordeaux, and in trying to regain the lost territories Henry proved as much a 'Softsword' as his father. His wars, coupled with his ambitious building and the grandiose style of his court, got him hopelessly into debt. His predictable solution – taxation – provoked the predictable response.

While Henry was formulating his lofty view of royal power, reform was in the air. The notion of a 'community of the realm' was taking shape among the thinking classes who were getting more numerous. Educated at the growing number of cathedral schools and in the colleges that were just starting up in the market towns of Oxford and Cambridge, the increasing ranks of graduates went into the Church for the most part. But some found work in the Exchequer and in the other developing offices of government, where the leading lights among the 'king's clerks' took pride in their work. They saw good and efficient government as an aim in itself, and they were starting to ask how this could be maintained when the King himself did not practise it?

The daring idea of controlling an unreliable monarch had been inherent in the thinking behind Magna Carta's twenty-five-strong watchdog committee, and as discontent mounted during Henry's long reign, calls grew to bring back this crucial feature of the Great Charter. By 1258 the fifty-one-year-old king was virtually bankrupt following an expensive foreign-policy adventure in which he had tried to make one of his sons king of Sicily. Now, under pressure from his barons, he finally gave way. Twelve of his nominees met at Oxford with twelve of the discontents to hammer out, Runnymede-style, how 'our kingdom shall be ordered, rectified, and reformed in keeping with what they think best to enact'.

The twenty-four-man think tank convened on 11 June 1258 at a moment of great national distress. The previous year's harvest had been catastrophic, and as the 'hungry month' of July approached, famine was becoming widespread. 'Owing to the shortage of food,' wrote Matthew Paris, 'an innumerable multitude of poor people died and dead bodies were found everywhere, swollen through famine and livid, lying by fives and sixes in pigsties and dunghills in the muddy streets.'

Extreme times produce extreme measures – in the summer of 1258, a 'New Deal' for England. The Provisions of Oxford which the twenty-four wise men produced that summer effectively transferred England's government from Henry to a 'Council of Fifteen'. These men would appoint the great officers of state, control the Exchequer, supervise the sheriffs and local officials, and have the power of 'advising the King in good faith regarding the government of the Kingdom'. The Provisions, which count alongside Magna Carta as milestones in England's constitutional history, were drawn up loyally in the name of the King. But they made a crucial distinction between the human fallibility of any par-ticular king and the superior institution of the Crown, whose job it was to guarantee the well-being of *all* the people, the 'community of the realm'.

One of the twenty-four wise men who had gathered at Oxford and subsequently a member of the Council of Fifteen was the Earl of Leicester, Simon de Montfort – a prickly and imperious Thomas Becket-like character, who, like Becket, began as his king's close friend but would end up as his nemesis. Years earlier, de Montfort had secretly wooed and won Henry III's sister, another Eleanor, and he was never afraid to take on his royal brother-in-law. The two men had savage stand-up rows in public, which de Montfort, with his overbearing manner, tended to win. Henry was rather in awe of him. Being rowed along the Thames one day, the King was overtaken by a thunderstorm and, terrified, ordered his watermen to make for the nearest landing-steps, which happened to belong to a house where de Montfort was staying. 'I fear the thunder and lightning beyond measure, I know,' the King candidly confessed as de Montfort came out to greet him. 'But by God's head, Sir Earl, I dread you even more.'

De Montfort came from northern France and had grown up in the same martial atmosphere as Richard the Lionheart. Like Richard, he went on crusade to the Holy Land, and distinguished himself there in battle. He was an inspiring general – and a pious one. He would frequently rise at midnight to spend the hours until dawn in silent vigil and prayer. His best friend was Robert Grosseteste, the Bishop of Lincoln, who wrote a treatise setting out the difference between good rule and tyranny. De Montfort, who had sipped self-righteousness, it sometimes seemed, with his mother's milk, came to believe over the years that his royal brother-in-law was little more than a coward and a tyrant. Furthermore, he had no doubt that he alone knew the way to achieve just rule.

In the aftermath of the Provisions of Oxford this unbending sense of morality stirred up trouble with de Montfort's fellow-barons. Why should the King alone be subject to outside controls? he asked. What about those barons and lords who abused their authority at the expense of the ordinary people? Needless to say, this was not at all what the barons wanted to hear. When the King, with their backing, enlisted the Pope to absolve him from his oath to the Provisions of Oxford, de Montfort's coalition fell apart. His critics had complained, with some justification, that he was not above exploiting his eminence for the benefit of his own family, and in October 1261 the earl stalked off to France in disgust, swearing never to return.

Less than two years later he was back. Henry had reverted to his bad old ways, and now his popularity was lower than ever. On one occasion when his wife tried to sail down the Thames in the royal barge, Londoners went to scoop up the manure that filled the streets in the days before sanitation and expressed their feelings by pelting the Queen with pungent missiles from London Bridge.

When de Montfort called for a restoration of the Provisions of Oxford, many rallied to his cause. Between 1263 and 1265 England was convulsed by civil war, with de Montfort championing the cause of reform. In May 1264, facing the royal army at Lewes on the Sussex Downs, he ordered his men to prostrate themselves, arms spread out in prayer, before donning armour that bore the holy crosses of the crusaders. The general himself, having injured his leg in a riding accident, had been transported to the battlefield in a cart. His forces were heavily outnumbered. But the rebels' fervour carried the day. De Montfort took the King's eldest son Edward (named after the Confessor) as a hostage, and set about putting the Provisions of Oxford into practice.

The Provisions had called for the regular summoning of 'parliament' – literally a 'talking-place' (from the French word *parler*, to speak) – and it was Simon de Montfort's Parliament of January 1265 that secured his place in history. This was by no means the first English parliament to be summoned. The term had been used in 1236 to describe the convention of barons, bishops and other worthies whom the King summoned to advise him – it was not unlike the old Anglo-Saxon *witan*, the council of wise men. But we should not think of this extended royal council as anything like our modern Parliament, with its own identity and its own permanent buildings. In the thirteenth century parliament was called at the king's pleasure, wherever he happened to be in the country – it was an event rather than an institution.

But in January 1265, for the first time, came two knights from every shire, along with two burgesses (town representatives) from York, Lincoln and other selected boroughs to parlay in London with the barons, bishops and clergy. Here was the seed of the modern body that now holds the ultimate political authority over our lives, and the gathering was invited to discuss a major question – what to do with Prince Edward, the King's son, whom Simon had taken hostage after the Battle of Lewes.

For townsfolk and country landowners to be conferring on the fate of a future king was heady stuff. In the climate of the times it could not last – and Simon's own followers took fright at the thought of meddling in such mighty matters. In the event, the twenty-five-year-old Edward escaped from captivity and took command of the royal forces, to confront the earl's depleted troops at Evesham that August. The outcome was a foregone conclusion.

'God have mercy on our souls,' cried the old general as the immensely larger royal army approached, 'for our bodies are theirs.'

Simon de Montfort was killed in the brief and bloody slaughter that followed. His testicles were cut off, to be hung around his nose, and his body was then dismembered, with his feet, head and hands being sent around the country as an object lesson to other rebels. But his dream did not die. What was left of him was buried at Evesham and became a place of pilgrimage. Miracles were reported, and songs were sung about this fearless, awkward, self-righteous French-born grandee, who had undoubtedly enriched himself in his campaigning, but who did at least have a vision of a fairer, more representative land.

'Simon, Simon, you are but sleeping,' sang the faithful. One day Simon would wake, went the dream, and with him the cause of liberty in England.

A PRINCE WHO SPEAKS NO WORD OF ENGLISH

AD 1284

IN MAY 1265 THE FUTURE KING EDWARD I WAS being held hostage in Hereford Castle. Since the Battle of Lewes the previous May his uncle Simon de Montfort had been detaining him under house arrest. It was a courteous kind of detention – the twenty-five-year-old prince was not actually a prisoner – so when a dealer brought some horses to the castle, his guards saw no harm in letting the young man try them out. The men walked him down to an open space, where he gave them a superb display of horsemanship. The athletic young man, over six feet tall, put each of the animals vigorously through its paces, wheeling, galloping, spurring them on and yanking them into sudden stops and turns, until all but one were exhausted. Then he sprang on to the last remaining fresh horse and rode off to freedom.

Shrewd calculation and physical prowess were the hallmarks of Edward I, who came to the throne in 1272. His father Henry III had managed the longest reign of any English sovereign yet, but had run the Crown's authority and its finances into the ground. So when Edward finally succeeded his father, he cannily presented himself as a reformer, ready to implement at least some of the parliamentary principles championed by de Montfort. Edward also looked beyond England, to the island's furthest shores, ambitious to win control of all Britain. It was this lofty aim that inspired one of the enduring stories of his reign.

The Normans had always laid theoretical claim to Wales, but the middle years of the thirteenth century had seen a series of native freedom fighters robustly dispute this. In Welsh they called themselves *tywysogion*, which in the official documents was translated into Latin as *principes*. So the English – their traditional enemies – described them as 'princes' of Wales. In a series of brilliant and brutal campaigns, Edward I defeated the last two Welsh 'princes' and ringed north-west Wales with a chain of massive stone castles which stand to this day. They represent the pinnacle of the castle-builder's art, and it was to the building-site that would be Caernarfon Castle, looking across at the island of Anglesey, that the King brought his pregnant wife Eleanor in the spring of 1284.

According to the story, Edward had promised the conquered Welsh that he would give them 'a prince born in Wales who speaks no word of English', and that April

Eleanor duly produced a son, another Edward. From the battlements of Caernarfon Castle, the proud father presented the Welsh with their newborn prince – who spoke not a word of anything. Tradition has it that, far from being insulted, the Welsh were thoroughly delighted by King Edward's little joke, and that from that day to this all heirs to the English throne have been called Princes of Wales.

That was the legend, first recorded some two hundred years later, and it is true that the baby prince was born in Wales. But there were no battlements at Caernarfon at that date, only some muddy excavations. More important, the new-born Edward of Caernarfon was not his father's heir – that distinction belonged to his eleven-year-old brother, Alfonso. It was not until 1301, after Alfonso's death, that, shortly before his seventeenth birthday, the future Edward II was declared Prince of Wales, and that was in Lincoln, just about as far from Caernarfon as you could get. When Edward became king, he did not name his own son, the future Edward III, Prince of Wales, and in the centuries that followed a number of heirs to the English throne were not given the title.

It was not until the twentieth century, in fact, that an heir to the English throne was invested as Prince of Wales *in Wales*. In 1911 the demagogic Welsh politician David Lloyd George invented a fake medieval ceremony especially for the purpose, complete with a striped 'crusader tent' and a princely costume that the seventeen-year-old future king, Edward VIII, described as a 'preposterous rig'. In 1969 Prince Charles wore a more conventional, military uniform, and the crusader tent was replaced by a transparent Perspex awning, the better to televise the pageant, which, commentators told millions of viewers around the world, had been inspired by King Edward I in 1284.

Edward Longshanks, as he was nicknamed, was a man of impressive capacity, a tall, lean warrior, every inch a king. Like his great-uncle the Lionheart, he went to Palestine as a crusader and displayed both bravery and an ability to organise. With him to the Holy Land he took his wife Eleanor, to whom he was deeply attached. When she died in Northamptonshire in 1290, the King mounted a procession to carry her back to London, marking the occasion by having a series of tall, highly decorated stone crosses built at every spot where the cortège stopped along the way. The last stopping-point before Westminster was in the neighbourhood of Charing, and a replica of the cross stands in front of Charing Cross Station in London today.

Edward was a man of ferocious temper, notorious for boxing the ears of his children when they displeased him. The royal account book lists repairs to his daughter Elizabeth's coronet in 1297, after he had hurled it into the fire. His tomb in Westminster Abbey bears the inscription *Malleus Scottorum*, the 'Hammer of the Scots'. But his attempts to conquer Scotland did not yield the success that he had enjoyed in Wales, and in a series of bloody campaigns he was held off by the Scottish heroes William 'Braveheart' Wallace and Robert the Bruce.

These setbacks did not deter his people from rating Edward I an English hero, and they even applauded the act of bigotry that is the enduring blot on his reputation to this day. In the course of his unsuccessful Scottish campaigns and his Welsh castle-building programmes, the King found himself in dire financial difficulties and he resorted to desperate measures. Monarchs such as Richard I had traditionally tried to protect England's Jewish communities of merchants and moneylenders against popular prejudice, but in 1290, in return for a large subsidy from Parliament, Edward I agreed to expel England's Jews. There were some three thousand, it has been estimated, living in about fifteen communities. Some were killed, many were robbed, and Edward himself took about £2000 in proceeds from the houses they were compelled to abandon.

It was the ugly face of the faith that had inspired Longshanks to go crusading. When a Jew, before the expulsion, went to Parliament to complain about the case of a Jewish boy who had been forcibly baptised a Christian, Edward did not see the problem. 'The king does not want to revoke the baptism,' reads the ledger. 'No enquiries are to be made of anyone, and nothing is to be done.'

It is a comment to ponder as you look at the beautiful Charing Cross.

PIERS GAVESTON AND
EDWARD II

AD 1308

'FAIR OF BODY AND GREAT OF STRENGTH',
Edward of Caernarfon, England's first Prince of Wales,
was widely welcomed when he came into his inheritance as
King Edward II at the age of twenty-three. But as he made
his way down the aisle of Westminster Abbey at the end of
February 1308 with his young queen Isabella, daughter of
the French king Philip IV, all eyes turned to the individual
behind him – Piers Gaveston, a young knight from Gascony.
The new king had awarded Gaveston pride of place in his
coronation procession, bestowing on him the honour of carrying the crown and sword of Edward the Confessor, and
Gaveston, in royal purple splashed with pearls, was certainly

dressed for the occasion. His finery was such, wrote one chronicler, that 'he more resembled the god Mars, than an ordinary mortal'. According to the gossips, King Edward was so fond of Gaveston that he had given him the pick of the presents that he had received at his recent wedding to Isabella. The Queen's relatives went back to France complaining that Edward loved Gaveston more than he loved his wife.

Edward's father, Edward I, the pugnacious 'Hammer of the Scots', had been infuriated by his son's closeness to the flamboyant young Gascon. The old king had made Gaveston, the son of a trusted knight, a ward in the prince's household, but there were complaints that the two men got up to mischief together, frequenting taverns and running up debts. On Edward I's last unsuccessful campaign against the Scots in Carlisle in the winter of 1306–7, the prince had suggested giving Gaveston some of the royal estates in France. His father exploded, seizing Edward by the hair and tearing it out in tufts. He ordered Gaveston into exile.

On coming to the throne, Edward II's first concern had been to expedite the return of his friend Piers. When he went off to France to marry Isabella in January 1308, a few weeks before the coronation, he placed Gaveston in charge of England, and, to the fury of just about every baron in the land, he also bestowed on him the rich earldom of Cornwall.

The reckless passion of Edward II for Piers Gaveston ranks as the first of the momentous love affairs that have shaken England's monarchy over the centuries. Homosexuality was deeply disapproved of in medieval England. It was considered by many a form of heresy – a ticket to hell – though there is enough evidence to make it clear that many a monk and priest might have been seen at the ticket barrier. 'The sin against nature' was usually referred to indirectly, with comparisons to the Old Testament love of King David for Jonathan – 'a love beyond the love of women'. When writing specifically of Edward's love for Gaveston, the chroniclers of the time would call it 'excessive', 'immoderate', 'beyond measure and reason'. But one source referred directly to a rumour going around England that 'the King loved an evil male sorcerer more than he did his wife, a most handsome lady and a very beautiful woman'.

It should be stressed that the details of Edward's physical relationship with Gaveston are as unknowable as those of any other royal bedchamber, and we should not forget that the King had four children by Isabella. It has even been argued that the two men were totally chaste, cultivating their relationship as devoted 'brothers'. Certainly, none of this would have been an issue if Edward had not allowed his private affections to intrude so fiercely into his public role. Other kings had no problems with same-sex relationships. It is generally assumed that William Rufus (who ruled from 1087 to 1100) was gay – he produced no children and kept no mistresses – and the same has been said of Richard Coeur de Lion, though this is hotly denied by recent biographers. Whatever their predilections, these monarchs did not allow their private passions to impinge on their royal style or, more important, to influence their decisions when it came to handing out land and other largesse.

Edward II, however, displayed an assortment of characteristics that were viewed as unkingly. For a start, he dressed like his friend Piers, a little too extravagantly. He enjoyed the unusual sport of swimming and also rowing, which was considered demeaning – kings traditionally showed their power by getting others to row *them*. He kept a camel in his stables. He pursued a whole range of 'common' pursuits such as digging, thatching, building walls and hedges, and he enjoyed hammering away at the anvil like a blacksmith. Nowadays England might welcome a DIY king, but in the fourteenth century such activities, not to mention the pleasure Edward took in hobnobbing with grooms and ploughmen, were considered abnormal.

The major grievance, however, was the disproportionate favour that Edward showed Piers Gaveston. When the barons in Parliament called for the exile of the favourite, Edward's response was to endow him with still more castles and manors. He did agree, reluctantly, that Gaveston should go over to Ireland for a while as his representative, but he was clearly unhinged by his departure. The King took his entire household to Bristol to wave Gaveston off and pined for him in his absence, getting personally involved in such petty problems as the punishment of trespassers on Gaveston's property on the Isle of Wight.

When, in an attempt to curb the King's aberrations, Parliament presented him with a set of 'Ordinances' in 1311, along the lines of Simon de Montfort's Provisions of Oxford, Edward took the extraordinary step of offering to agree to any restriction on his own powers provided that his favourite was in no way affected.

The muscular Gaveston did not make things any easier. He took delight in defeating the barons in jousts and tournaments, and then rubbed salt in their wounds by mimicking his critics and giving them derisive nicknames. The Earl of Gloucester was 'whoreson', Leicester was 'the fiddler', and Warwick the 'black hound of Arden'.

'Let him call me"hound",' the earl exclaimed. 'One day the hound will bite him.'

As approved by Parliament and reluctantly agreed by the King, the Ordinances of 1311 imposed stringent controls on royal power. Building on Magna Carta and the Provisions of Oxford, championed by Simon de Montfort, it was now laid down that the King could not leave the kingdom without the consent of the barons, and that parliaments must be held at least once or twice a year and in a convenient place. Clearly, the immediate purpose of the Ordinances was to deal with Gaveston, who was promptly sent out of the country for a second time. But he sneaked quietly back, and by the end of November there were reports of the favourite 'hiding and wandering from place to place in the counties of Cornwall, Devon, Somerset and Dorset'. That Christmas he appeared openly at Edward's side at Windsor.

For the indignant barons, this act of defiance was the last straw. Using the authority of the Ordinances, they summoned troops, while Edward and Gaveston headed north to rally forces of their own. Cornered at Newcastle, they managed to escape, Edward to York and Gaveston to Scarborough, where the barons besieged him. Lacking supplies, Gaveston surrendered, and under promise of safe conduct he was escorted south. But just beyond Banbury the party was ambushed by the Earl of Warwick, who whisked the favourite back to his castle and delivered the promised 'bite'. On 19 June 1312, Piers Gaveston was beheaded at Blacklow Hill on the road between Warwick and Kenilworth.

The killing of Edward II's beloved 'brother' devastated the King and prompted a backlash of sympathy in his favour. But two years later, finally doing what a king was supposed to do and leading his army north against Scotland, Edward was heavily defeated between Edinburgh and Sterling in June 1314. Robert the Bruce's brave and cunning victory at Bannockburn is one of the great tales of Scottish history, but in England its consequence was a massive further blow to Edward's authority. Early in 1316 at the Parliament of Lincoln, the King humbly agreed to hand over the running of the country to the barons.

The trouble was that Edward had found himself another Gaveston. Hugh Despenser was an ambitious young courtier whose father, also named Hugh, had been an adviser and official to Edward I and still wielded considerable power. The Despensers came from the Welsh borders or Marches, and they used their influence shamelessly to extend their lands. Once again the barons found themselves rallying together to restrict the power of a royal *familiaris* – a favourite – and this time a new element came into play. In 1325 Edward's long-suffering wife Isabella seized the chance of a journey to France to take a stand against the husband who had humiliated her, first with Gaveston and now with the younger Despenser. She took a lover, Roger Mortimer, another powerful Welsh Marcher lord, who had taken up arms against the King and the Despensers in 1322, and who, after being imprisoned in the Tower of London, had been lucky to escape to France with his life.

When Mortimer and Isabella landed in England in 1326, they had only a few hundred men, but they held a trump card – Isabella's elder son by Edward, the thirteen-year-old Prince Edward. As heir to the throne, the boy represented some sort of hope for the future, and London welcomed the Queen, whose cause, according to one chronicler, was supported by 'the whole community of the realm'. In a widespread uprising, the hated Despensers were tracked down and executed – in the case of Edward's favourite, at the top of a ladder in Hereford, where his genitals were hacked off and burned in front of his eyes.

England now set about doing something it had never attempted before – the deposition of a king by legal process. Prelates prepared the way. Early in January, the Bishop of Hereford preached to a clamorous London congregation on the text 'a foolish king shall ruin his people', and a parliament of bishops, barons, judges, knights and burgesses was convened in Westminster. Preaching to them on 15 January 1327, the Archbishop of Canterbury took as his text '*Vox populi, Vox dei*' – 'The voice of the people is the voice of God.' By the unanimous consent of all the lords, clergy and people, he announced, King Edward II was deposed from his royal dignity, 'never more to govern the people of England', and he would be succeeded by his first-born son, the Lord Edward. So Edward III would be the first English monarch appointed by a popular decision in Parliament.

It remained to break the news to the King himself, then imprisoned at Kenilworth Castle, and a deputation of lords, churchmen, knights and townsfolk set off forthwith for the Midlands. Dramatically clad in black, Edward half fainted as he heard William Trussell, a Lancastrian knight, read out the verdict of the whole Parliament. It grieved him, he said in response, that his people should be so exasperated with him as to wish to reject his rule, but he would bow to their will, since his son was being accepted in his place. Next day Trussell, on behalf of the whole kingdom, renounced all homage and allegiance to Edward of Caernarfon, and the steward of the royal household broke his staff of office, as if the King had died. The deputation returned to Parliament and the new reign was declared on 25 January 1327.

Now formally a non-king, Edward was imprisoned in the forlorn and ponderous Berkeley Castle overlooking the River Severn just north of Bristol. It is possible that, with time, his imprisonment might have been eased so as to allow him to potter around the grounds, digging his beloved ditches and hammering out a horseshoe or two. But in the space of just a few months there were two attempts to rescue him, and the Queen's lover, Mortimer, decided that he was too dangerous to be left alive. In September 1327 a messenger took instructions down to Berkeley, and two weeks later it was announced that Edward of Caernarfon, only forty-three and of previously robust health, was dead. Abbots, knights and burgesses were brought from Bristol and Gloucester to view the body, and they reported seeing no visible marks of violence. Edward had had 'internal trouble' during the night, they were informed.

But in the village of Berkeley, tales were told of hideous screams ringing out from the castle on the night of 21 September, and some years later one John Trevisa, who had been a boy at the time, revealed what had actually happened. Trevisa had grown up to take holy orders and become chaplain and confessor to the King's jailer, Thomas, Lord Berkeley, so he was well placed to solve the mystery. There were no marks of illness or violence to the King's body, he wrote, because Edward was killed 'with a hoote brooche [meat-roasting spit] putte thro the secret place posterialle'.

A PRINCE WINS HIS SPURS

AD 1346

IN THE AUTUMN OF 1330 THE BARONS WERE summoned to a Parliament in Nottingham. The writs went out in the name of the king, but everyone knew that the eighteen-year-old Edward III was not really running the country. Control over the young monarch was lodged firmly in the hands of his mother's lover, Roger Mortimer, who had awarded himself an earldom in his three years of power since the deposition of Edward II – along with land and money that he flaunted extravagantly.

Mortimer's ruthless elimination of his enemies had made him widely feared, and when the barons rode into Nottingham they found themselves under the forbidding eye of the earl's Welsh archers, stationed in the battlements of the castle up on the rocks above the River Trent. Inside the castle were Mortimer, Queen Isabella and the young king, on whom Mortimer kept a close eye.

Unknown to the earl, however, the rocks on which the castle stood were warrened with caves and crevices, and Edward had a plan that would cut short his tutelage. On the night of Friday 19 October 1330 a group of lords crept into the fortress via a secret passage. Waiting there for them was the young King who led them to Mortimer's chamber where, according to one source, he himself struck down the door with a battle-axe. As they finished off the two knights who were guarding the earl, the Queen rushed into the room.

'Bel fitz! Bel fitz!' she cried. 'Ayez pitié du gentil Mortimer!' – 'Fair son, fair son, have pity on sweet Mortimer!'

Her cries went unheeded, and the raiding party hustled the 'sweet' earl back down through the secret passage below the rocks, leaving his archers none the wiser up on the battlements. Next day Edward III proclaimed himself fully king and started off back to London, where Mortimer was found guilty on a string of charges that included the murder of Edward II. On 29 November the earl was hanged as a common criminal beneath the elms at Tyburn, having been spared the more hideous penalties of 'drawing' (disembowelling) and quartering that were prescribed by law for treason. Edward also showed restraint towards his mother Isabella, despatching her to comfortable retirement at Castle Rising in Norfolk and sending her, the royal accounts reveal, a steady flow of treats – a wild boar for roasting, a pair of lovebirds which she fed on hemp seeds, and generous quantities of wine from Gascony.

Decisiveness and generosity, delivered in style, were the hallmarks of the reign of Edward III. He was one of England's most dynamic monarchs, and much of his energy was devoted to war – specifically the conflict which history textbooks would later call the 'Hundred Years War'. In reality, this was a series of wars that lasted more than a hundred years, growing out of England's claims to lands in France – and at this moment in the 1330s, from a dispute over the rich territory of Gascony which Henry II had acquired nearly two centuries earlier through his marriage to Eleanor of Aquitaine.

Nestling in the south-west of France, just above the Pyrenees, Gascony was a prosperous region that produced revenue for the English king, largely on the strength of its subtle and cheering red *vin claret* ('clear wine'). In the four-teenth century the English drank more claret from the Gascon vineyards of Bordeaux than we do today, per head of the population, and the Gascons, who spoke their own lan-guage, liked their profitable relationship with England. Its distant kings threatened less interference than did the French kings in Paris, who had pushed the English out of Normandy and Anjou and were now nibbling away at the English holdings in south-west France. There had been a series of skirmishes involving the *bastides*, the walled towns along Gascony's borders, and in May 1337 King Philip VI went the whole hog. He announced that he was confiscating all Gascon territories – to which Edward III responded by restating his claim to the French throne itself through his mother Isabella.

Edward had enjoyed remarkable military success since

seizing power in 1330. He was a charismatic leader, strikingly handsome with a pointed yellow beard – he had 'the face of a God', according to one contemporary. A fan of jousting, he was constantly honing his own warlike skills in tournaments, along with those of the men around him, who came to form the tough core of his military campaigns. Starting in Scotland, he had reversed the inept record of his father with a spectacular victory at Halidon Hill, near Berwick on the banks of the Tweed, where the firestorm of arrows from the English and Welsh longbowmen shattered the Scots.

The two-metre longbow, both longer and heavier than the bows that had been used at Hastings, was to revolutionise military tactics in the fourteenth century. The English encountered it when fighting the Welsh, whose capacity to pierce chain mail and even a thick oak door with their iron-tipped arrows had been mightily impressive. In his enthusiasm, Edward I had called for villagers to practise archery every Sunday and holy day, and Parliament passed laws forbidding tennis, dice and cock-fighting as well as various forms of cricket and hockey (described as 'club-ball') because they diverted men from their target practice. Football was particularly disapproved of, as leading to hooliganism and riots.

In contrast, French laws prohibited peasants from possessing any arms at all. French military tactics still centred on the mounted knight, and the difference showed when the French and English armies met on the battlefield of Crécy near the French Channel coast in 1346. The French far outnumbered the English, by nearly thirty thousand to ten or fifteen thousand according to one estimate, with the French forces including some six thousand Genoese mercenaries wielding crossbows. A formidable weapon made of wood banded with iron – almost a machine – the crossbow fired a lethal bolt with great velocity and had a greater range than the longbow. But while a crossbow archer could load and trigger off only four bolts in a minute, the much more flexible longbowman could fire eight or even ten arrows in the same time. The French knights, furthermore, despised the foreign mercenaries that their King had engaged, and even rode down their own crossbowmen at one stage in the battle.

The entire outcome of Crécy seems to have been determined by the arrogance of the French horsemen. The 'flower of France', as the knights liked to call themselves, arrived in front of the English position on the hill of Crécy on the evening of 26 August 1346. Raring for battle, they ignored their king's orders to halt and make camp for the night. The sun was setting as they charged up the hill, and under their onslaught the English archers wasted not a single arrow. If they did not strike riders, they struck horses, wreaking havoc. According to Jean le Bel, one of the chroniclers of the battle, the dead and wounded horses piled on top of one another 'like a litter of piglets'.

As the French recoiled in confusion, they were struck by another of Edward III's secret weapons – Welsh and Cornish knifemen, armed only with daggers. Their speciality was to creep under the enemy's horses and cut open their bellies, and they took advantage of the dusk to slink up and 'murder many [men] as they lay on the ground, both earls, barons, knights and squires'.

It was not till the sun rose the next morning that the

English realised what a massive victory they had achieved. Edward III sent out his heralds – the clerks who were experts in coats of arms – and, picking their way through the corpses on the battlefield, they identified more than fifteen hundred slain lords and knights, in addition, perhaps, to some ten thousand enemy footsoldiers and crossbowmen, who, unlike the knights, were not counted. Among the dead lay John, the blind King of Bohemia, who had brought his troops to support the French and had ordered his knights to lead him forward, 'so that I may strike one stroke with my sword'. The discovery of his corpse, still tied to the bodies of his knights by their reins, became one of the legends of the victory.

The other concerned Edward's son, the sixteen-year-old Edward Prince of Wales, said to have worn black armour. Thrown to the ground by the French charge, the 'Black Prince' was rescued by his standard-bearer, who covered his body with the banner of Wales. Messengers asking for help were sent post-haste to Edward, who had set up his headquarters in a windmill overlooking the field, but the King refused. 'Let the boy win his spurs,' he said, 'for I want him, please God, to have all the glory.'

When help did reach the prince, they found him with his standard-bearer and companions 'leaning on lances and swords, taking breath and resting quietly on long mounds of corpses, waiting for the enemy who had withdrawn'. Someone had brought from the battlefield the crest of the King of Bohemia, three tall white ostrich plumes, and the prince took them as his badge there and then. He also adopted the blind hero's motto, which Princes of Wales bear to this day – *Ich Dien*, 'I serve.'

THE BURGHERS OF CALAIS

AD 1347

THE ENGLISH VICTORY AT CRÉCY ASTONISHED
Europe. 'Nobody thought much of the English, nobody
spoke of their prowess or courage,' wrote the chronicler Jean
le Bel. 'Now, in the time of the noble Edward, who has often
put them to the test, they are the finest and most daring
warriors known to man.'

It was less, in truth, a matter of personalities than of military technology. The light, mobile bowmen of England and
Wales, trained on their village greens and selected at archery
contests, had challenged the superiority of the mounted
knight – and, fortunately for England, it took the French a
remarkably long time to work it out. Edward III, by contrast,

was a canny leader, and he proved it after Crécy when he decided to head north towards Calais.

The English king understood that, if he was to maintain his position in France, he needed a secure deep-water port on the French side of the Channel. Visible from Dover on a clear day, Calais would give him a stranglehold on the sea-lanes, with a chance of controlling both trade and the growing problem of freelance piracy. Edward knew marching from Crécy to Paris to besiege the French capital would have been a step too far, whereas making Calais an English port would yield a solid dividend from his victory.

Calais, however, was not going to give in without a struggle. The port had strong natural defences of sand dunes and marshes, and as a walled town it was not just a centre of trade but had a semi-military status. It was customary for medieval rulers to provide incentives for communities to live in strategic fortresses on the understanding that they would make it their job to defend the fortress when it was attacked. This meant, in turn, that the men, women and children of a fortress town like Calais were treated as combatants if an enemy besieged them. They could expect no mercy if their resistance was breached.

Edward settled down for a long siege. Gunpowder was just making its appearance in European warfare, but the primitive cannon of the time had neither the range nor the power to demolish town walls. Out of range of the defenders' crossbow fire, Edward now built his own settlement of wooden huts, and to brighten up the winter he brought over his wife and the ladies of the court. The English king enjoyed female company, and he had encouraged his men to bring their wives, too. In addition, merchants came twice a week from Flanders to hold markets in the English camp.

Inside Calais itself, however, life was not so comfortable. In the early months of the siege, the inhabitants succeeded in smuggling in supplies by sea. But Edward was able to block-ade the harbour mouth, and in late June 1347, nearly a year after the siege had begun, the English defeated a French convoy that had tried to break through with supplies. In the wreckage was found an axe head that had been thrown over-board to avoid capture. Attached to it was a desperate message that the town's governor, Sir John de Vienne, had intended for the King of France:

> *Know, dread Sir, that your people in Calais have eaten their horses, dogs, and rats, and nothing remains for them to live upon unless they eat one another. Wherefore, most honourable Sir if we have not speedy succour, the town is lost!*

Edward III read the document, sealed it with his own seal and sent it on to its destination.

When, four weeks later, King Philip of France finally appeared with his army on the sand dunes within sight of Calais, cheers and sounding trumpets were heard from inside the town. The King's banner with the fleur-de-lis was run up on the castle tower, and the famished inhabitants lit a great fire. But on the second night the fire was somewhat less, and on the third night, after no rescue, it was just a flicker. Wails and groans were heard from inside the walls.

The French king had camped at Sangatte, notorious at the beginning of the twenty-first century as the site from which thousands of foreign immigrants smuggled themselves illegally into Britain – but Philip did not have their appetite for penetrating the English defences. After taking a good look at Edward's impressive encampment and the rested, well supplied English troops, he decided to retreat.

The following day Sir John de Vienne appeared on the battlements offering to negotiate, and shortly afterwards, barely able to hold himself erect, he rode out of the gates on a starving, wasted horse, to surrender his sword and the keys of the city. Round his neck the governor wore a rope, offering himself up to be hanged; and behind, roped to him, straggled a bizarre procession – the leading knights and burghers of the town, emaciated and in tatters, offering their own lives so that those of their fellow-citizens might be saved.

Edward acted mercifully – up to a point. One chronicler says that it was his wife, Philippa of Hainault, who persuaded him to spare the burghers of Calais. But on 4 August 1347 the English king entered the town with his soldiers and ordered the evacuation of virtually all the inhabitants, whose property he confiscated. To replace them, he shipped a colony of settlers over from England and built a ring of forts around the town. Calais would remain English for more than two hundred years.

THE FAIR MAID OF KENT AND
THE ORDER OF THE GARTER

AD 1347–9

SEEKING DIVERSION DURING THE ELEVEN long months that he was camped outside Calais, King Edward III held a grand ball to celebrate the victory at Crécy. The ladies of the court were decked out in all their finery, but as they danced, one of them lost her garter, the elegant circlet of blue silk that was holding up one of her stockings. It fell to the floor, and the King, in expansive mood, picked it up and tied it round his own well shaped leg.

Edward III's flamboyant gesture has gone down in history, though it was only recorded a century later. If the lady in question had been his wife, there would have been no special reason for comment. But Queen Philippa was pregnant at the time. She may not have been at the ball or she may have been sitting out the dancing. What is certain is that the soldier king had an eye for the ladies, and in 1347, according to some historians, his fancy had alighted on the great beauty of the day, Joan of Kent, wife of the Earl of Salisbury.

Although she was only nineteen, this remarkable young woman had already managed to acquire two husbands at once. This same year the 'Fair Maid of Kent' was embroiled in a bigamy case, and was faced with having to explain to the Pope how and why she had married an earl when she was already married to a knight. The Pope's judgement was that she should return to her first husband, Sir Thomas Holland, and Joan seems to have made the best of it. She had five children with Holland before he died in 1360. The next year, she and the Black Prince, then thirty-one, fell in love and married (and had two children of their own, one of them the future King Richard II). The 'Fair Maid of Kent' would be the first beautiful and controversial Princess of Wales.

In 1347 much of this lay in the future, but the lady whose blue silk garter the king had snaffled was clearly a figure of such interest that eyebrows were raised – and Edward must have felt that some comment was required. '*Honi soit qui mal y pense*,' he declared in his medieval French, which is usually translated as 'Shame on him who thinks shameful thoughts.' But the message could be simply interpreted – 'No sniggering, please.'

Back at Windsor the following year, Edward III made the blue silk garter the focus of an extraordinary ceremony, when he founded an order of chivalry – the Order of the Garter – a brotherhood of just twenty-four knights who would serve the King as a veritable Round Table. Four years earlier

Edward had staged a Round Table dinner at Windsor, and now he formalised the idea of himself as a latter-day King Arthur, who was firmly established by this date as an English folk hero.

The myth of Arthur had been extensively popularised over the previous two hundred years by the writings of Geoffrey of Monmouth, a Welsh priest living in Oxford whose *Historia Regum Britanniae*, 'History of the Kings of Britain', became the bestselling English history book of the Middle Ages. No less than 220 handwritten copies survive to this day. Geoffrey incorporated the Welsh traditions of Merlin the Magician into the Arthur legend, setting it within the mainstream of Britain's story and going back to the days of Albion when the island, he claimed, was inhabited by giants.

Geoffrey's fanciful stories were denounced in his lifetime by more orthodox chroniclers as 'shameless and impudent lies', and there were a good number of those, starting with the giants. But his history was rather like a modern television docudrama, weaving facts with fantasy. His fables of the legendary British kings Lear (probably derived from a folk tale) and Cymbeline (based on a pre-Roman British chieftain Cunobelinus) were to inspire William Shakespeare, and Geoffrey's entire saga caught the imagination of a community growing conscious of itself and searching for a sense of national purpose and identity.

This was exactly what Edward III wished to harness with his Order of the Garter. In the months after his return from Crécy, he took his Round Table show on the road in a series of tournaments held at Windsor, Reading, Eltham, Canterbury, Bury and Lichfield. Here was all the fun of the fair, with tents and flags and trampled grass, stalls laden with food and drink, lords and ladies showing off and the populace watching and cheering. The tournaments were a travelling victory celebration for the stunning conquests in France – national morale-boosters to get people smiling for when the tax collectors next came knocking.

The King added one extra touch: in 1349 he held the first formal meeting of his new order on 23 April, St George's Day, adopting the dragon-slaying saint brought back by the crusaders. The pious and anaemic St Edward the Confessor, a reasonably genuine Englishman, continued to preside at Westminster Abbey, but out at Windsor the chapel of the Garter brotherhood was dedicated to George, the warrior Turk. Edward called his knights 'The Fraternity of St George', and it is from this date that people started thinking of St George as the patron saint of England.

Edward's knightly fraternity, England's first gentlemen's club, was copied across Europe. France tried the short-lived Order of the Star, the Dukes of Burgundy the more durable Order of the Golden Fleece, and today there is not a country in the world, whether republic or monarchy, without its medal-and-ribbon-bedecked honours system. The Order of Lenin, the Order of the Chrysanthemum, the Order of the Elephant – all are solemn and thoroughly self-important institutions. How very English of Edward III to apply a name that injected humour, with a touch of scandal, into the country's ultimate social distinction. You might even imagine, as the King's eyes twinkled across the dance floor at the Fair Maid of Kent, that he was making fun of the whole ridiculous business.

THE GREAT MORTALITY

AD 1348-9

A S ENGLAND CELEBRATED ALL THROUGH the heady victory summer of 1348, a merchant ship from Gascony was docking in the port of Melcombe in Weymouth Bay. It was 23 June, the eve of St John, celebrated across the country as a fertility festival, when the village maidens dressed in their finery and bonfires were lit. But, disembarking from the vessel with the crew, to be borne along the drovers' paths and through the marketplaces of the ripening Dorset countryside, were the germs of an island-wide disaster.

In later centuries it was called the Black Death. At the time people talked of 'the Pestilence' or 'the Great Mortality'.

Either way, the imagery was dark enough. 'We see death coming into our midst like black smoke,' wrote the Welsh poet Euan Gethin, 'a plague which cuts off the young, a root-less phenomenon which has no mercy for fair countenance.'

Gethin himself was laid low by the infection, like one third of the five million or so other inhabitants of England and Wales, and he described the ghastly symptoms:

> *Woe is me of the shilling in the armpit. It is seething, terrible, wherever it may come, a head that gives pain and causes a loud cry, a burden carried under the arms, a painful angry knob, a white lump. It is of the form of an apple, like the head of an onion, a small boil that spares no one. Great is its seething, like a burn-ing cinder, a grievous thing of an ashy colour.*

It would be more than five centuries before the plague bacillus was isolated and identified by the French bacteriol-ogist Alexandre Yersin in 1894 – hence its name, *Yersinia pestis*. But its contagious nature was recognised from the start. In 1346 Mongol forces besieging the Black Sea port of Caffa lobbed the bodies of their plague victims over the walls into the city – an early example of biological warfare. It was trade that had brought the infection from the East, and in at least two varieties. Pneumonic plague was spread on the breath from contaminated lungs, and resulted in a ghastly choking death, with bloody froth bubbling at the mouth. Bubonic plague was spread by fleas and by the black rat, *Rattus rattus*, an agile creature that could run up and down the mooring ropes of ships. One symptom of the disease was ravening hunger in both flea and rat, which made them the more likely to bite. As the rats scurried along the rafters and through the thatched roofs of fourteenth-century England, the infected fleas would drop down off their backs on to the humans below.

The symptoms of plague were swollen lymph nodes in the armpits and groin known as buboes – Euan Gethin's apples and onions – and death followed within hours, or a few days at most. Victims suffered from bad breath – 'a loathsome, cadaverous stink from within', according to one contemporary, and other symptoms included high fever, acute stomach pains and bluish-black spots on the body.

'The sick are served by their kinsfolk as dogs would be,' wrote one chronicler. 'Food is put near the bed for the sick to eat or drink, after which all fly.' Another related how 'fathers and mothers refused to see and tend their children, as if they had not been theirs'.

It was not surprising that such a trauma induced agonised soul-searching across the whole of Europe. When King Philip VI of France demanded an official explanation from the medical faculty of the University of Paris, he was told that God, in his anger, had ordained a fatal conjunction of the planets. This had sucked up the waters of the sea, creating an invisible but lethal 'miasma' (from the Greek word for 'pollution' or 'defilement'), a poisonous cloud that infected all who inhaled it.

Divine retribution also figured heavily in England's diagnosis, with the monkish chroniclers pointing a finger at the debauchery that went on at the royal tournaments. Between jousts the crowds would be entertained by female cheerleaders, some of them dressed like men in tight-fitting costumes that showed off their figures.

'We are not constant in faith,' complained Thomas Brinton, the great preacher who thundered his denunciations from the pulpit of Rochester Cathedral in Kent in the 1370s and '80s. 'We are not honourable in the eyes of the world.'

Not even the King himself was spared. Edward III's second daughter Joan, barely thirteen years old, was struck down in Bordeaux that September. She was on her way to Spain to marry Pedro, the heir to the kingdom of Castile, and had been travelling with her dowry, which included her own huge red silk marriage bed.

'No fellow human being could be surprised,' wrote Edward to King Alfonso, as one father to another, 'if we were inwardly desolated by the sting of this bitter grief, for we are human too.'

After the initial attack of 1348 and 1349, the plague returned to England five more times before the century was out – in 1361, 1368, 1374, 1379 and 1390. The fall-out was catastrophic, seeping into every aspect of life, from the way the land was farmed, after a third – or even a half – of the workforce had been smitten, to the relaxation of regulations governing feudal service and marriage: fewer tenants, fewer spouses, fewer rules. Grasping at the notion that the plague was an airborne 'miasma', more houses were now fitted with closed windows, shutters and heavy tapestries, while frequent bathing went out of fashion: the hot water was thought to open the pores to airborne infection.

Recent medical research shows that some effects of the Black Death have lasted into present times. Doctors researching the AIDS epidemic have discovered that there are certain, relatively rare, people who will never come down with AIDS, however much they are exposed to it. What these people have in common has been identified as a gene mutation known as CCR5-delta 32, found mostly in white Europeans and especially in Swedes. Doctors suspect that the ancestors of these people were precisely those who were infected and managed to survive the plagues of the fourteenth century. The mutation does not appear to exist in African and East Asian populations that did not suffer the Black Death.

Bubonic plague – identified by its underarm swellings – still exists today. It can be treated with antibiotics if diagnosed early enough, but two thousand deaths are reported worldwide each year, and a recent case in Madagascar showed a worrying resistance to antibiotics. AIDS, SARS, deadly influenza epidemics – the plagues are still with us.

THE BEDSIDE MANNER OF
A PLAGUE DOCTOR

AD 1376

JOHN ARDERNE MADE HIS REPUTATION BY devising a treatment for an embarrassing ailment that was suffered by many in the age of chivalry. Knights spent hours, days, even months in the saddle – the mounted heroes of Crécy bumped their bottoms all the way to France and back. *Fistula in ano*, an unpleasant abscess between the base of the spine and the anus, was an occupational hazard of their apparently glamorous profession, and Arderne developed a surgical technique for treating it. He cut out the abscess, using opiates to deaden the pain, and wrote up his method in a precisely illustrated treatise of 1376 that ranks as one of the earliest professional medical articles. The basic principles of his treatment are followed by surgeons to this day.

Arderne learned his craft as a doctor by tending to the wounds of English soldiers in the French wars, and he favoured experimentation. He prided himself on knowing better than the old medical dogmas dating back to Greek times, though he did acknowledge that he had made some mistakes early on. On one occasion he tried sprinkling leg wounds with powdered arsenic that ate away at the bone. Fortunately for Arderne, suing for compensation was not yet a national pastime. People were well aware they could die in almost any medical situation, and were grateful for whatever help the doctor could give them.

After the failure of his arsenic powder, Arderne concocted gentler dressings using mutton fat, which he christened *salus populi*, the 'balm of the people', and he came to specialise in herbal remedies. His remedy for gout was a poultice of green laurel and honey mixed with the lard of a male pig – he claimed to have cured a gouty abbot overnight with a single application – and his remedy for kidney stones was a plaster of pigeon's dung and honey applied hot to the body. These cures might sound outlandish to modern ears, but his patients came back for more, and the astrological spells that he used while dispensing his treatments seem to have had a calming effect. One of his most popular was a charm he originally came up with to tackle the hangovers suffered by the guests who caroused too freely at the wedding of Lionel, the Black Prince's younger brother. The hangover cure worked so well he tried it for epilepsy, and reported success.

The good doctor should not boast, advised Arderne, nor

should he pass comment on his colleagues. It was better to err on the safe side when discussing prospects of recovery, and he should always be modest and discreet. Also, he should always keep his nails clean. When it came to fees, the rich should be charged as much as possible – high fees inspired their confidence – and while the poor should be treated free as a matter of professional prestige, there was no harm done if they provided the odd chicken or duck.

When attending the bedside, there was nothing wrong in deploying a little flattery, and better still if the doctor could tell a few good stories that would make the patient laugh. It induced anxiety in a patient if the physician took his relatives aside to whisper in a corner, nor should he be too familiar with 'fair women in great men's houses'. He should certainly avoid greeting them in public by thrusting his hands about their bosoms – which would seem, on the face of it, to raise the question of what form a private greeting from the jolly Dr Arderne might take.

When it came to the plague, Arderne did not pretend to have a solution. He offered patients who suffered from heart attacks an expensive cure that involved gold dust and a powder made from pearls. But he advised his colleagues to try to avoid hopeless cases as a matter of principle. An honest doctor risked losing his fee *and* his reputation – and, worse, could find himself accused of poisoning.

John Arderne was proudest of the remedies he devised for the battlefield, and particularly a salve for arrow wounds that he called '*sangue d'amour*' – the blood of love. This ideally required the blood of a maiden aged twenty, drawn at the full moon in Virgo (mid-August to mid-September).

It would then be mixed with myrrh, aloes and other ingre-dients before being boiled up with olive oil. But the doctor had confected a red powder to take the place of the maiden's blood – 'for now,' he explained, 'in this time, virgins come full seldom to twenty years'.

THE DREAM OF PIERS THE PLOUGHMAN

AD 1377

One summer season when the sun was warm, I rigged myself out in shaggy woollen clothes as if I were a shepherd; and in the garb of an easy-living hermit I set out to roam far and wide through the world, hoping to hear of marvels. But on a morning in May, among the Malvern Hills, a strange thing happened to me, as though by magic. For I was tired out by my wanderings, and as I lay down to rest under a broad bank by the side of the stream, and leaned over gazing into the water, it sounded so pleasant that I fell asleep. And I dreamt a marvellous dream . . .

S O BEGINS PIERS THE PLOUGHMAN, A RAMBLING
epic poem that takes a stroll through plague-stricken
England in the declining years of Edward III. We read of
monks and friars, proud barons and burgesses in fur-
trimmed coats, poor parish priests who can no longer scrape
a living from their death-diminished parishes, and, of course,
a ploughman. Piers is a brave, plain-spoken innocent, a good-
hearted man of the people, who seeks to make sense of the
world.

Piers the Ploughman was the life's work of William
Langland, a quirky and impoverished churchman who spent
many years working and reworking his saga, his one and
only known creation, in colloquial verse. Langland grew up
in the Malvern Hills in Worcestershire where his first 'vision'
is set, but then moved to London to scratch a living by
singing masses for the souls of the rich and transcribing legal
documents. He must have had some difficulty in supporting
his wife Kit and their daughter Collette in their cottage in
Cornhill, between London Bridge and the modern Bank of
England. He himself features prominently in the poem – he
is the dreamer – and the poem is the source for just about all
that we know about him. 'Long Will' describes himself as
tall, lean and disrespectful. He sometimes dressed in rags
like a beggar so that he could experience the life of the poor,
and when he encountered pompous or self-important people
he would take pride in being disrespectful.

In his very first vision, Langland dreams of a gathering of
rats and mice that are terrified of an overbearing cat who is
playfully batting them about – 'scratching and clawing us
and trapping us between his paws until our lives are not

worth living'. At the suggestion of one elderly rat they solemnly debate the old folk-fable idea of securing a bell to the monster's collar in order to protect themselves against it, but end up with the famous dilemma – 'Who will bell the cat?'

'Now what this dream means,' says Langland, 'you folk must guess for yourselves, for I haven't the courage to tell you.'

The guess was an easy one for Langland's fourteenth-century readers. The poet was referring to the parliaments of his time. The cat was the King – the ageing and ailing Edward III, on the throne for more than half a century. The rats and mice were the knights and burgesses who made up Parliament.

After Crécy, the war with France had gone well for a while. In 1356 the Black Prince, who had taken over England's armies on behalf of his father, won a brilliant victory at Poitiers against all the odds. The French King John II was actually captured and held to ransom. But since 1369 it had been all downhill, with retreats and loss of territories. The Black Prince fell ill, and the senile Edward III had fallen under the influence, since the death of his wife Philippa, of his mistress Alice Perrers. The royal demands for taxes kept on coming, and all this amid the strain and turmoil of the Black Death.

In 1376 the 'Good Parliament', as they boldly called themselves, had tried to stop the rot. They elected themselves a Speaker – Parliament's first – who presided over business that included scathing attacks on royal ministers and favourites, Alice Perrers among them. The Commons expected the King to 'live off his own', they declared, and

not to assume he could just go on squeezing his people –
hence the wise old rat's idea of a 'bell'. But no sooner had
Parliament broken up than the 'cat', in the form of Edward's
younger son John of Gaunt, had had the Speaker arrested
and the Acts of the Good Parliament annulled.

'Even if we kill the cat,' remarks one of Langland's mice
cynically, 'another like him would come to scratch us, and it
would be no use our creeping under the benches. I advise all
commoners to leave him alone and let's not be so rash as
even to show him the bell.'

Piers the Ploughman was less a political tract than a spiritual
adventure. Langland's vision was that life's purpose is the
seeking of truth, and that truth when explored turns out,
rather beautifully, to be the same as love, dwelling in the
human heart. But this unconventional man who dressed as a
beggar to sample the life of the disadvantaged had a keen eye
for injustice, and there are angry passages in his poem that
give us a unique view of how some people lived in late
fourteenth-century England:

> *The poorest folk are our neighbours if we look about us – the pris-*
> *oners in dungeons and the poor in their hovels, overburdened with*
> *children, and rack-rented by landlords. For whatever they save by*
> *spinning they spend on rent, or on milk and oatmeal to make gruel*
> *and fill the bellies of their children who clamour for food. And they*
> *themselves are often famished with hunger, and wretched with the*
> *miseries of winter – cold sleepless nights, when they get up to rock*
> *the cradle cramped in a corner and rise before dawn to card and*
> *comb the wool, to wash and scrub and mend . . .*

There are many more who suffer like them – men who go hungry and thirsty all day long, and strive their utmost to hide it – ashamed to beg, or tell their neighbours of their need. I've seen enough of the world to know how they suffer, these men who have many children and no means but their trade to clothe and feed them. For many hands are waiting to grasp the few pence they earn, and while the friars feast on roast venison, they have bread and thin ale, with perhaps a scrap of cold meat or stale fish.

In the story of *Piers the Ploughman,* as in the brief poem of Caedmon the cowherd, we get a rare chance to hear the early voice of an ordinary Englishman – transfused in Langland's case with a burning anger. It would not be long before this voice of the people – and their anger – would be more loudly heard.

THE 'MAD MULTITUDE'

AD 1381

When Adam delved and Eve span
Who was then a gentleman?

JOHN BALL'S QUESTIONING AND PROVOCATIVE couplet excited the crowds gathered on the green heights of Blackheath overlooking London in the early summer of 1381. As the fiery preacher conjured up the image of Adam, the original man, painfully delving— or digging – in the fields, while his wife laboured with her spindle in their mud-and-wattle hovel, twisting piles of sheep's wool into yarn, his audience knew exactly what he was getting at.

'In the beginning,' cried Ball, 'all men were equal. Servitude of man to man was introduced by the unjust dealings of the wicked. For if God had intended some to be servants and others lords, He would have made a distinction between them at the beginning.'

John Ball's sermon was inspired by a plague-stricken land. His restive audience had dutifully obeyed both the lord of the manor and their Lord in heaven, and they had been punished with death – in 1348, 1361, 1368, 1374 and again five years later. But they also had a self-confidence and assertiveness they had not known before, since, by the brutal laws of economics, the survivors of the plague years were actually better off than they had ever been. A drastically reduced labour force meant higher wages – and if you could scrape together some savings, you could also pick up land cheaply. Modern archaeologists have noticed how smart metal utensils began to replace earthenware pots in quite ordinary homes during these years. Higher living standards, lower rents, a more diversified economy – all this from a flea on a rat's back. And with these changes came a resonating cry for social justice.

'What can they show,' asked Ball, 'or what reasons give why they should be more the masters than ourselves? Except, perhaps, in making us labour and work, for them to spend.'

The Great Rising of 1381 sought to break the cycle of feudal bondage, the system whereby men gave their labour and their loyalty – and, in many ways, their very being – to the local lord of the manor in return for land and protection. For this reason later generations called the uprising the Peasants' Revolt.

But to judge from the records, it might better have been

called the Ratepayers' Revolt, since the ledgers of the time show that the leaders and mouthpieces of the rebellion like John Ball, Wat Tyler and Jack Straw were substantial, tax-paying folk. Anything but peasants, they came from the upwardly mobile yeoman classes. They were village leaders who sat on juries – and their rebellion first exploded not in the poor and downtrodden areas of England but in the very richest counties, the fruitful orchards of Kent and Essex, close to London with its alluring wealth and progressive ideas.

Discontent had been stirred by a general conviction that things were awry at the top. Edward III had died in 1377, after the debacle of the 'Good Parliament', leaving the throne to his ten-year-old grandson Richard II. 'I heard my father say,' remarked one of William Langland's dream mice, 'that when the cat is a kitten the court is a sorry place.'

While Richard was a child, the court was in the hands of his uncle John of Gaunt, so named because he was born during a royal visit to Ghent in the Low Countries. Gaunt lacked the charisma of his elder brother, Richard's father, the Black Prince, whose premature death was the more mourned because he was widely thought to be a reformer – and Gaunt positively prided himself on his lack of the common touch. 'Do they think that they are kings and princes in this land?' he had asked as he annulled the reforms of the Good Parliament. 'Have they forgotten how powerful I am?'

Gaunt had maintained the dreary pursuit of war with France and Scotland, and the huge expenditure that this necessitated had kept the tax demands coming. The final provocation was the poll tax of 1380 – the third in four years. 'Poll' meant 'head' (thus counting per head, the same word we use for elections), and it was a new way of raising money. Previously, taxes had been levelled per household. They were known as 'tenths', 'thirteenths' or 'fifteenths', reflecting the fraction of your household wealth you were expected to pay. Now people were supposed to pay according to the number of heads polled in their homes – which automatically doubled your tax burden if you were married, and increased it still more if you had parents living with you, or children over the age of fourteen.

Not surprisingly, many people had conveniently 'lost' members of their family when the tax collectors called. Between 1377 and 1381, the Exchequer was faced with a mysterious fall of 33 per cent in the adult population, and correctly suspecting tax evasion, the government sent out fresh teams of examiners, with powers of arrest and escorts of armed guards, to root out the hidden evaders.

It was the arrival of one such commission in the Essex town of Brentwood at the end of May 1381 that provided the spark for rebellion. Led by John Bampton, the local Member of Parliament, the commissioners started summoning representatives from the area to account for the deficits in their payments. But those from the villages of Fobbing, Corringham and Stanford-le-Hope felt they were being threatened. They refused to cooperate, and when Bampton's armed escort attempted to arrest the villagers there was uproar. The tax commissioners were expelled from Brentwood, and Bampton fled to London in fear for his life.

Within days, much of Essex had risen in rebellion. Several

thousand protesters headed for London, while down in Kent the standard of revolt was flown by Wat Tyler, who then lived in Maidstone but had earlier lived in Essex. Tyler may have been a link between the surprisingly well coordinated uprisings now occurring in these counties to the north-east and south-east of the capital.

On Monday 10 June, Tyler led some four thousand rebels to Canterbury, where they broke into the cathedral during the celebration of high mass, demanding that the monks depose the Archbishop Simon Sudbury. Sudbury was a leading member of the government, and Tyler's followers denounced him as 'a traitor who will be beheaded for his iniquity'. During these years, radical religious thinking was marching in step with social revolution. The Oxford philosopher John Wycliffe was teaching that men could find their own path to God without the help of priests, whose riches, power and worldliness he denounced. His followers, most of them from poor backgrounds, were called Lollards – literally, in Middle English, 'mumblers', a reference to their constant mouthing of their own private prayers to God.

When the rebels got to London they soon tracked down Archbishop Sudbury, who was hiding in the Tower along with Sir Robert Hales, the King's treasurer. Both men were dragged out, to be beheaded by the crowds, who paraded their severed heads on poles in a triumphant procession to Westminster Abbey. In the bloody mayhem that followed, the protesters looked for more scapegoats – and found them in the immigrant merchant communities from Flanders and Lombardy, who had taken over royal money-raising from the Jews. It was lucky for John of Gaunt that he was away from London on yet another military campaign. But the mass looted his sumptuous palace by the Thames anyway, and even cornered the King's mother, Joan, and asked her to kiss them. Now an elderly lady, the Fair Maid of Kent, whose beauty was said to have inspired the Order of the Garter all those years before, fainted clean away from the shock.

The one member of the court to rise bravely to the occasion turned out to be the 'kitten' – the fourteen-year-old King Richard II. On Saturday 15 June 1381, the boy rode out to the north-west of the city to the meadows of Smithfield, London's meat market then as now. A small but self-assured figure, he was accompanied by about two hundred courtiers and men-at-arms, facing a much larger party of rebels on the other side of the field.

Wat Tyler came riding proudly out from the rebel ranks on a little horse, a lone figure, with just a dagger in his hand for protection. As he dismounted, he half bent his knee and took the boy king's hand in a rough and jocular fashion. 'Brother,' he said, 'be of good comfort and joyful!'

The rallying cry of the masses as they marched towards London had been 'For King Richard and the true commons!', for they nursed the fantasy attending the monarchy to this day that, personally, the monarch is somehow without fault. Royal mistakes are the fault of royal advisers and, at heart, the monarch is the people's friend – 'We shall be good companions,' Tyler promised the king.

Richard evidently bridled at this familiarity. 'Why will you not go back to your own country?' he asked – by 'country' he meant Tyler's own place or neighbourhood – and at this rejection, the rebel leader flared up angrily. Neither he nor his companions would leave, he swore vehemently, until they had got agreement to their demands. He then launched into his manifesto:

'There should be equality among all people,' he proclaimed, 'save only the king . . . There should be no more "villeins" in England, and no serfdom or villeinage.' All men should be 'free and of one condition' – and when it came to the Church, all its worldly goods should be confiscated. A reasonable amount should be set aside to provide the clergy with 'sufficient sustenance', but the remaining church property should be divided among the people of the parish.

It was a wish list of breathtaking idealism and impossibility, bolder than any Englishman has ever demanded face to face with his king. If Tyler really did deliver the people's demands with the fluency and power with which the chronicler wrote it down, he was a man of remarkable eloquence and courage. He seems to have been the key to the revolt – and what happened next has been fiercely debated by historians. Was there a prearranged plan to set Wat Tyler up, or was it his own arrogance that provoked the denouement?

According to one chronicler, he concluded his great speech by calling for a flagon of water, then 'rinsed his mouth in a very rude and disgusting fashion' in Richard's face. According to another, he was tossing his dagger from hand to hand 'as a child might play with it, and looked as though he might suddenly seize the opportunity to stab the king'.

Tyler was 'the greatest thief and robber in all Kent,' called out one of the royal retainers, thereby provoking the rebel leader – as was perhaps the intention – to lunge at his accuser with his dagger. When the Mayor of London intervened, Tyler started to stab him, and would have injured him severely if the mayor had not been wearing armour beneath his costume – another clue that the royal party had come to Smithfield ready for trouble.

It was all the royal bodyguard needed. One promptly fell on Tyler, running him through with his sword. Mortally wounded, Tyler pulled himself up on to his horse and headed back towards his comrades. Then, crying out for help, he fell to the ground in the no man's land separating the two sides. Angry archers in the watching rebel ranks began to flex their bows, and were only prevented from loosing their arrows by the sight of the boy King himself, spurring his horse forward and calling out to them with a personal appeal – they should come with him to the nearby fields of Clerkenwell, he cried, for further discussion.

Even allowing for the exaggeration of loyal chroniclers, Richard's bravery and presence of mind were remarkable. He defused a moment that could have led to wholesale bloodshed, and his composure turned the tide which, until then, had been flowing in the rebels' favour.

Wat Tyler's followers took their grievously wounded leader to the nearby St Bartholomew's Hospital, but the mayor had him dragged out and beheaded. No one stepped forward to take Tyler's place, and the men of Kent – 'enveloped', as one observer put it, 'like sheep within a pen' – allowed themselves to be ushered homewards over London Bridge.

The great revolt continued to rage in other parts of the country. In St Albans, Cambridge and Bury St Edmunds, merchants and craftsmen rose to free their towns from the control of local abbeys, fighting for the right to function as independent communities. In Norfolk men rose up in town and countryside alike. But at the end of June royal troops advanced on Essex and mercilessly crushed all resistance they encountered. According to one chronicle, five hundred men perished. More reliable figures indicate that some thirty-one ringleaders were identified, tried and hanged on the gallows.

'Rustics you were and rustics you are still,' declared the young Richard later, on his tour of Essex. 'You will remain in bondage, not as before, but incomparably harsher.'

The juvenile hero of Smithfield rescinded every concession he had granted under the pressure of rebellion – in his value system, promises made under duress did not count. The blithe courage that he had shown at Smithfield sprang from the mantle of divine appointment in which he would wrap himself for the rest of his reign. John Ball and Jack Straw were tracked down, tried and hanged, and in a Parliament that was summoned at the end of the year the knights, gentlemen and burgesses wasted no time in reaffirming the social restrictions that had provoked the uprising in the first place. Now that it was safe again to sneer, the rebels with their high-flown ideas of freedom and equality were dismissed as 'the mad multitude'.

But Parliament never again tried a poll tax – well, at least not for another six hundred and nine years, when Margaret Thatcher's Conservative government imposed a 'per head' community charge on a reluctant country. Once again the electoral rolls displayed mysterious 'disappearances' – 130,000 names went missing in London alone – and once again the protesters came to the capital to fight pitched battles in the streets. In 1990, however, the rebels got their way. Mrs Thatcher was jettisoned by her colleagues – for their own survival. Her successor John Major wasted no time in dropping the poll tax, and was returned to power in the next general election.

The processes of democracy and consultation that we enjoy today saw their origins in the years whose story is told in this book. From the wise men who advised the Anglo-Saxon kings, via the first 'social contract' reluctantly agreed by the hapless Ethelred the Unready, the green shoots of freedom had started to flourish. The Norman Conquest seemed a setback, but that too enriched England's cross-bred culture, not least her potent, subtle language – some of the most English things about England, we discover, have come from abroad.

In the Peasants' Revolt we have heard cries for liberty and equality that resound to this day, and we have seen those demands brutally suppressed. Two steps forward, one step back. The economic power that the Black Death paradoxically shifted in the direction of ordinary working people would prove with time to be a key engine for change in the future. We have not yet heard much about women, tolerance, science, playwrights, walking on the moon, comfort or safety. Kings, warriors and ghastly beheadings have loomed considerably larger in our story than they will in future volumes. But, as we 'take a break' in 1381, monarchs and wars are not over – and nor are the beheadings.

BIBLIOGRAPHY AND
SOURCE NOTES

GENERAL HISTORIES OF ENGLAND

Single-volume histories of England were out of fashion for many years, but have staged a glorious revival with Roy Strong's *The Story of Britain* – with Norman Davies in *The Isles* providing a healthily subversive corrective to Anglocentric tendencies. Listed below are the other general histories that I have consulted, and I recommend all of them, from Charles Dickens's romantic Victorian overview to the eye-witness accounts collected by John Carey. *The Oxford Companion to British History* is the ideal general reference work, and Alison Weir's *Britain's Royal Families* contains every conceivable date relating to England's kings and queens. Christopher Lee's *This Sceptred Isle* is built around some well chosen extracts from Churchill's *History of the English-speaking Peoples*, but there is nothing like the real thing. Ackroyd and Scruton provide personal interpretations from the heart. Fernández-Armesto looks at the bigger picture.

Our Island Story by H. E. Marshall is long out of print, but an American edition of 1920 has been lovingly digitalised and put on the Net by the Celebration of Women Writers project hosted by the University of Pennsylvania. It can be viewed in its entirety, with its illustrations, on www.digital.library.upenn.edu/women/marshall/england/england.html.

Ackroyd, Peter, *Albion: The Origins of the British Imagination* (London, Chatto & Windus), 2002.
Brewer's Dictionary of Phrase and Fable, Millennium Edition (London, Cassell), 2001.

Carey, John (ed.), *The Faber Book of Reportage* (London, Faber and Faber), 1987.

Churchill, Winston S., *A History of the English-speaking Peoples*, 4 volumes, Birth of Britain (London, Cassell), 2002.

Davies, Norman, *The Isles: A History* (London, Papermac), 2000.

Diamond, Jared, *Guns, Germs and Steel* (London, Vintage), 1998.

Dickens, Charles, *A Child's History of England*, (Oxford, Oxford University Press), 1998.

Fernández-Armesto, Felipe, *Truth – A History and a Guide for the Perplexed* (London, Black Swan), 1998.

Johnson, Paul, *The Offshore Islanders: A History of the English People* (London, Phoenix), 1998.

Lee, Christopher, *This Sceptred Isle 55BC–1901* (London, Penguin Books), 1997.

The Oxford Companion to British History, rev. and ed. John Cannon (Oxford, Oxford University Press), 2002.

Rogers, Everett M., *Diffusion of Innovations* (New York, The Free Press), 1995.

Schama, Simon, *A History of Britain*, 3 volumes (London, BBC Worldwide), 2001–2.

Scruton, Roger, *England – an Elegy* (London, Pimlico), 2001.

Strong, Roy, *The Story of Britain: A People's History* (London, Pimlico), 1998.

Strong, Roy, *The Spirit of Britain: A Narrative History of the Arts* (London, Pimlico), 2000.

Weir, Alison, *Britain's Royal Families: The Complete Genealogy* (London, Pimlico), 2002.

Wood, Michael, *In Search of England: Journeys into the English Past* (London, Penguin Books), 2000.

FURTHER READING AND PLACES TO VISIT

Simon Schama's landmark TV series *A History of Britain* has now been accompanied by a guidebook to the historical sites shown on screen –

and to many more. It opens with Iron Age villages and the Avebury stone circles and progresses to the great castles of Edward I. English Heritage and the National Trust are the two principal custodians of our historic treasures, whose details are set out on their websites: www.English-Heritage.org.uk; www.nationaltrust.org.uk.

Davidson, Martin, *A Visitor's Guide to A History of Britain* (London, BBC Worldwide), 2002.

c.7150 BC: *Cheddar Man*

The bones of Cheddar Man can be seen at the Natural History Museum in London. There is a replica of his skeleton at Gough's Cave in Cheddar, Somerset, part of the exhibition 'Cheddar Man and the Cannibals': www.cheddarcaves.co.uk. See www.ucl.ac.uk/boxgrove for details of the excavation of Britain's very earliest human remains, the half-million-year-old legbone found at Boxgrove in Sussex. As this book went to press, English Heritage announced the exciting discovery of delicate engravings in the caves at Cresswell Crags near Worksop in Nottinghamshire, dating from around 10,000 BC – so our hunter-gatherer ancestors, it seems, had art! Catherine Hills offers an accessible and scholarly account of our country's earliest waves of uninvited immigrants.

Hills, Catherine, *Blood of the British: From Ice Age to Norman Conquest* (London, George Philip with Channel 4), 1986.

c.325 BC: *Pytheas and the Painted People*

In *The Extraordinary Voyage of Pytheas the Greek*, Barry Cunliffe pulls together the fragments of our knowledge about this remarkable man, taking us by the hand on a delightful stroll through Celtic Gaul and Britain. If you would like to visit Stonehenge on the summer solstice in the company of modern Druids, ring the English Heritage hotline on 0870 333 1186. Paul Newman writes well about the prancing white horses on the hills.

Chadwick, Nora, *The Celts* (London, Penguin Books), 1997.

Cunliffe, Barry, *The Extraordinary Voyage of Pytheas the Greek* (London, Penguin Books), 2002.

Delaney, Frank, *The Celts* (London, HarperCollins), 1993.

Newman, Paul, *Lost Gods of Albion: The Chalk Hill Figures of Britain* (Trowbridge, Sutton Publishing), 1999.

55 BC: *The Standard-bearer of the 10th*

You can't do better than read Julius Caesar's own story of hitting Britain's beaches, contained in his account of his campaigns in Gaul.

Caesar, Julius, *The Gallic War*, trans. Carolyn Hammond (Oxford, Oxford University Press), 1996.

AD 1–33: *And Did Those Feet? Jesus Christ and the Legends of Glastonbury*

Michael Wood's poetic work of reportage *In Search of England* (see General Histories, above) tackles the fantasies of Glastonbury gently but firmly. For the sacred, visit www.glastonburyabbey.com. For the profane, you can find out about the annual pop music festival on www.glastonburyfestivals.co.uk.

AD 43: *The Emperor Claudius Triumphant*

Barbara Levick's recent biography paints a sympathetic portrait of the crippled emperor. You can find out how to visit the Roman remains at Colchester at www.colchestermuseums.org.uk.

Levick, Barbara, *Claudius* (London, Routledge), 2002.

AD 61: *Boadicea, Warrior Queen*

Shrewdly separating fact from fiction, Antonia Fraser refers to the warrior queen as Boudicca when dealing with verifiable events, and as Boadicea when legend takes over. Tacitus's *Annals* provides an almost contemporary version of the revolt. His *Agricola* tells us what his father-in-law, the Roman governor, did next, while his *Germany* describes the Germanic tribes whose descendants would eventually cross the seas to fill the void left by the Romans. The Museum of London has a standing exhibit on what happened when Boadicea came to town: www.museum-london.org.uk. Colchester is looking for volunteers to take part in its annual Boadicea chariot race on www.colchesterfestival.org.

Fraser, Antonia, *The Warrior Queens: Boadicea's Chariot* (London, Phoenix), 2002.

Tacitus, *Annals of Imperial Rome*, trans. and intro. Michael Grant, rev. edn (London, Penguin Books), 1996.

Tacitus, *Agricola and Germany*, trans. and intro. Anthony R. Birley, (Oxford, Oxford University Press), 1999.

Webster, Graham, *Boudica: The British Revolt against Rome*, AD 60 (London, B. T. Batsford), 1993.

AD 122: *Hadrian's Wall*

After many years of restoration, Rome's great English pleasure palace is now open again at Bath: www.romanbaths.co.uk. To visit Hadrian's Wall, consult www.hadrians-wall.org.

Drinkwater, J. F., and Drummond, A., *The World of the Romans* (London, Cassell), 1993.

Potter, T. W., and Johns, C., *Roman Britain* (London, British Museum Press), 1992.

AD 410–c.600: *Arthur, Once and Future King*

Enter 'King Arthur' in your search engine and more than a million pages will vie to take you back to Camelot. So read the man who started it all – the twelfth-century chronicler Geoffrey of Monmouth, in accessible paperback. Of the real-life Arthurian sites, Tintagel Castle in Cornwall comes closest to what Hollywood would lead you to expect. For a genuine and spectacular taste of the Dark Ages, you have the choice of the British Museum or the Sutton Hoo burial site in Suffolk to see *Beowulf* brought to life: www.thebritishmuseum.ac.uk; www.suttonhoo.org

Barber, Richard, *King Arthur, Hero and Legend* (Woodbridge, Boydell Press), 1961.

Carver, Martin, *Sutton Hoo, Burial Ground of Kings?* (London, British Museum Press), 1998.

Monmouth, Geoffrey of, *The History of the Kings of Britain*, trans. Lewis Thorpe (London, Penguin Books), 1966.

c.AD 575: *Pope Gregory's Angels*

Here is our first chance to sample the writing of Bede, who tells the story of the Angles in the slave market, complete with Gregory's excruciating puns. An earlier but briefer account of the encounter can be found in the *Life* of Gregory by an anonymous monk of Whitby. According to this account, when the slaves told Gregory they were '*Angli*' (Angles), he replied that they were '*angeli Dei*' – 'angels of god'.

Bede, *Ecclesiastical History of the English People* (trans. Leo Sherley-Price, intro. D. H. Farmer), (London, Penguin Books), 1990.

AD 597: *St Augustine's Magic*

After describing Augustine's arrival in Canterbury, Bede went on to relate how the pagan altars around England became Christian. Maps showing the spread of Christianity in Anglo-Saxon England are among the many original features of David Hill's indispensable atlas. The original St Augustine's throne has long vanished, but if you visit Canterbury you can see the marble chair made in the early 1200s that stands near Thomas Becket's shrine.

Hill, David, *An Atlas of Anglo-Saxon England* (Toronto, University of Toronto Press), 1981.

AD 664: *King Oswy and the Crown of Thorns*

The gothic ruins of the Abbey of Whitby will be familiar to devotees of *Dracula* – Bram Stoker wrote his famous novel looking up at it. Today you can look down from the abbey on to the bracing sea view enjoyed by the guests of St Hilda at the synod in 664.

Legend has it that the migrating geese who rest on the headland on their way down from the Arctic every year are pilgrims paying tribute to her memory: www.whitby.co.uk.

c.AD 680: *Caedmon, The First English Poet*

You can read Caedmon's 'Hymn' in the gem-like anthology of Anglo-Saxon verse compiled by the poet Kevin Crossley-Holland, together with the complete text of *Beowulf*, *The Dream of the Rood* and a bawdy collection of Anglo-Saxon riddles. Seamus Heaney's translation of *Beowulf* has been rightly praised.

Crossley-Holland, Kevin (ed. and trans.), *The Anglo-Saxon World: An Anthology* (Oxford, Oxford University Press), 1984.
Heaney, Seamus, *Beowulf* (London, Faber and Faber), 1999.

AD 672/3–735: *The Venerable Bede*

www.bedesworld.co.uk offers a flavour of the old monastery at Jarrow, with visitor information. If you can't get to the north-east, the British Library video, *The Lindisfarne Gospels* (written by BL experts and narrated by Kevin Whateley of *Inspector Morse* fame) is atmospheric on monasticism in this period. Brown and de Hamel provide well illustrated accounts of how the writing studios at such monasteries produced their masterpieces. *The Age of Bede* sets out some good contemporary sources. Bede himself would surely be delighted by the cultural renaissance of modern Tyneside – his spirit is now said by some locals to flit between Durham Cathedral, where his bones rest, and Anthony Gormley's magnificent statue, the *Angel of the North*, in Gateshead.

Brown, Michelle P., *Anglo-Saxon Manuscripts* (London, The British Library), 1991.
de Hamel, Christopher, *Medieval Craftsmen: Scribes and Illuminators* (London, British Museum Press), 1997.
Webb, J. F. (trans.), Farmer, D. H. (intro.), *The Age of Bede* (London, Penguin), 1998.

AD 878: *Alfred and the Cakes*

Start with the original, Bishop Asser's *Life of King Alfred*. Then turn to the much criticised Alfred Smyth, who maintains that Asser was a forgery. There is not much marshland left in the Somerset Levels these days, but you can get a feeling of how the waters once swirled around the sedge when you look out from the train between Taunton and Bruton on a wet winter's day. On summer afternoons, you can climb up the great tower built at Athelney in the eighteenth century to commemorate Alfred's adventures in the swamps. That other great Anglo-Saxon king of the previous century, Offa of Mercia, left more of a memorial in the shape of his massive earthwork built to keep out the Welsh. Offa's Dyke Centre is at Knighton in Powys, halfway along the eighty-mile border trail: www.offasdyke.demon.co.uk.

Jones, Gwyn, *The Vikings* (London, The Folio Society), 1997.

Keynes, Simon, and Lapidge, Michael (trans.), *Alfred the Great: Asser's Life of King Alfred and Other Contemporary Sources* (London, Penguin Books), 1983.

Smyth, Alfred P., *King Alfred the Great* (Oxford, Oxford University Press), 1995.

AD 911–18: *The Lady of the Mercians*

From this point onwards, and for the next two centuries, we can enjoy the acerbic comments of the compilers of the *Anglo-Saxon Chronicle*. Kathleen Herbert, Henrietta Leyser and Pauline Stafford examine from different angles the role of women in medieval society.

Herbert, Kathleen, *Peace-Weavers and Shield-Maidens: Women in Early English Society* (Hockwold-cum-Wilton, Anglo-Saxon Books), 1997.

Leyser, Henrietta, *Medieval Women* (London, Phoenix), 1997.

Stafford, Pauline, *Queen Emma and Queen Edith: Queenship and Women's Power in Eleventh-century England* (Oxford, Blackwell Publishers), 1997.

Swanton, Michael (trans. and ed.), *The Anglo-Saxon Chronicle* (London, J. M. Dent), 1997.

AD 978–1016: *Ethelred the Unready*

Corfe Castle in Dorset, the site of the killing of Ethelred's half-brother Edward, is all that a castle should be, with a history of warfare that extends as late as the Civil War of the 1640s – see www.corfe-castle.co.uk. Lavelle's recent biography bravely defends the Unready's reputation. Michael Swanton's anthology contains Archbishop Wulfstan's famous denunciation of the evils of the reign of Ethelred – the Sermon of the Wolf to the English. To get a glimpse of the life created by the Danes whom Ethelred tried to slaughter, head for Jorvik (York to us), the place that a surprising number of Vikings called home: www.jorvik-viking-centre.co.uk.

Lavelle, Ryan, *Aethelred II: King of the English 978–1016* (Stroud, Tempus), 2002.

Swanton, Michael (trans. and ed.), *Anglo-Saxon Prose* (London, J. M. Dent), 1993.

c.AD 1010: *Elmer the Flying Monk*

Elmer went by many names in the documents –Aethelmaer, Eilmer, Aylmer and even Oliver – all derived from readings and misreadings of the original account of his flight by his fellow-monk William of Malmesbury. At Malmesbury Abbey the Friends of the Abbey bookshop sells a full account of the flight, including the researches of Dr Lynn White Jr, President of the US Society for the History of Technology. If you want the Friends to send you a copy of the book you will have to send them a book of stamps, since they do not have credit card facilities.

Malmesbury, William of, *Gesta Regum Anglorum*, *The History of the English Kings*, volume 2, general intro. and commentary by R. M. Thomson with M. Winterbottom (Oxford, Clarendon Press), 1999.

Woosnam, Maxwell, *Eilmer, Eleventh-century Monk of Malmesbury: The Flight and the Comet* (Malmesbury, Friends of Malmesbury Abbey), 1986.

AD 1016–35: *King Canute and the Waves*

Few of King Canute's attempts to make himself an English gentleman have survived. The story of how he tried to turn back the waves provides a great opportunity to dip into Henry of Huntingdon, the first of the post-Norman chroniclers to come our way. Lawson provides a thorough review of the original sources.

Huntingdon, Henry of, *The History of the English People 1000–1154*, trans. Diana Greenway (Oxford, Oxford University Press), 2002.

Lawson, M. K., *Cnut: The Danes in England in the Early Eleventh Century* (London, Longman), 1993.

AD 1042–66: *Edward the Confessor*

The Westminster Abbey that we see today was started in the reign of Henry III, but it is the obvious place to experience the dream of the Confessor. Make sure you visit the cloisters beside the abbey to get the flavour of the monastic buildings attached to the great church. The abbey's website is particularly rich in historical detail and displays an interpretation of what the Confessor's original abbey probably looked like: www.westminster-abbey.org. Debby Banham offers a wonderful insight into the everyday life of mid-eleventh-century monks through an analysis of the sign language they used when they were not allowed to speak – 'Pass my underpants, please.'

Banham, Debby (ed. and trans.), *Monasteriales Indicia: The Anglo-Saxon Monastic Sign Language* (Hockwold-cum-Wilton, Anglo-Saxon Books), 1996.

c.AD 1043: *The Legend of Lady Godiva*

Call up 'Godiva' on your search engine and you will have difficulty finding the strictly historical sites. The Harvard professor Daniel

Donoghue has written a stimulating analysis of the Godiva legend, which includes a translated text of Roger of Wendover.

Donoghue, Daniel, *Lady Godiva: A Literary History of the Legend* (Oxford, Blackwell Publishing), 2003.

AD 1066: *The Year of Three Kings*

Tracking the most graphic evidence for the events leading up to the Battle of Hastings requires a trip across the Channel to Bayeux in Normandy: www.bayeux-tourism.com. But almost better than a visit, Martin Foys's new CD-Rom enables you to scroll the whole tapestry and magnify images so that individual stitches can be seen, and compare the modern images with the facsimiles of the past. On www.hastings1066.com you can view the tapestry for nothing. From 1066 onwards, Nigel Saul delivers measured guidance to all the major events and themes.

Foys, Martin K., *The Bayeux Tapestry Digital Edition* (Woodbridge, Boydell & Brewer), 2003.
Saul, Nigel, *A Companion to Medieval England, 1066–1485* (Stroud, Tempus), 2000.
Howarth, David, *1066: The Year of the Conquest* (New York, Penguin Books), 1981.

AD 1066: *The Death of Brave King Harold*

Battle Abbey in East Sussex – said to be built on the very spot where Harold's body was found – is open the year round and English Heritage guides will show you round the famous battlefield. The pioneering work of David Hill and John McSween has yet to be published but is summarised, with some illustrations, in Lawson's exhaustive study.

Hill, David, and McSween, John, *The Bayeux Tapestry: The Establishment of a Text*, forthcoming.
Lawson, M. K., *The Battle of Hastings, 1066* (Stroud, Tempus), 2002.

AD 1070: *Hereward the Wake and the Norman Yoke*

Once again, Michael Wood (see General Histories, above) is the most readable. His account of the Norman Yoke starts memorably with his encounter as a teenager with the great general, Montgomery of Alamein – with Clement Attlee playing a supporting role. Castle websites abound. Start with www.castles.org and www.castles-abbeys.co.uk. And if you missed Marc Morris's television series, don't miss his book.

Morris, Marc, *Castle* (London, Channel 4), 2003.

AD 1086: *The Domesday Book*

The Public Record Office was recently rebranded as the National Archives. It remains an airy temple of documentary delights. There is a small exhibition room on the ground floor where you can view Domesday in its glass case, in the company of a changing selection of themed exhibits: www.nationalarchives.gov.uk.

Hallam, Elizabeth, *Domesday: Souvenir Guide* (London, Public Record Office), 1986.

AD 1100: *The Mysterious Death of William Rufus*

You can visit William Rufus's magnificent banqueting hall in the Palace of Westminster – www.parliament.uk/parliament/guide/palace.htm. To get the flavour of a Norman royal hunting preserve, visit the New Forest in Hampshire – ideally with a copy of Duncan Grinnell-Milne's book, which treats William Rufus's killing in the style of a murder mystery. The Yale English Monarchs series provides consistently excellent biographies of all the medieval kings, but try Brooke for a single volume overview, which is particularly perceptive on Rufus's death.

Brooke, Christopher, *The Saxon and Norman Kings* (London, Fontana), 1984.

Grinnell-Milne, Duncan, *The Killing of William Rufus: An Investigation in the New Forest* (Newton Abbot, David & Charles), 1968.

AD 1120: *Henry I and the* White Ship
Once again a trip to Normandy is in order. From the lighthouse on the cliffs beside Barfleur you can see the rock on which the *White Ship* foundered. The account by Orderic Vitalis is one of the most gripping passages in any of the medieval chronicles.

Chibnall, Marjorie (trans. and ed.), *The Ecclesiastical History of Orderic Vitalis*, volume 6, Books XI, XII and XIII (Oxford, Clarendon Press), 1978.

AD 1135–54: *Stephen and Matilda*
This is where we say goodbye to the *Anglo-Saxon Chronicle*, whose description of the civil war horrors around Peterborough provides a rousing, if tragic, conclusion.

Davis, R. H. C., *King Stephen 1135–1154* (London, Longman), 1990.

AD 1170: *Murder in the Cathedral* and AD 1174: *A King Repents*
The stunning stained-glass windows in Canterbury Cathedral's Trinity Chapel, which were created within half a century of Thomas Becket's death, tell the story of his murder and the miracles that followed. Henry VIII tried his best to eradicate the cult of St Thomas in the sixteenth century, but the aura of the martyr survives. Frank Barlow's study of Becket is a particularly fine biography.

Barlow, Frank, *Thomas Becket* (London, The Folio Society), 2002.

AD 1172: *The River-bank Take-away*
You can read the full text of William FitzStephen's description of London in Frank Stenton's Historical Association leaflet. The Museum of London is the place to go for imaginative exhibits on the medieval city: www.museum-london.org.uk.

Stenton, Frank, *Norman London, An Essay* (London, Historical Association), 1934.

AD 1189–99: *Richard the Lionheart*

Coeur de Lion has been well served by his biographers, with John Gillingham the most notable. Should you be lucky enough to go sailing down the River Danube, look out for the site of Richard's imprisonment, Castle Durnstein, the archetypal wicked baron's fortress. Lying buried side by side in Fontevrault Abbey by the River Loire, Richard and his parents, Henry II and Eleanor of Aquitaine, make a poignant family scene.

Gillingham, John, *Richard the Lionheart* (London, Yale), 1999.

Nelson, Janet L. (ed.), *Richard Coeur de Lion in History and Myth*, Medieval History series (London, King's College), 1992.

Phillips, Jonathan, *The Crusades 1095–1197* (Harlow, Pearson Education), 2002.

AD 1215: *John Lackland and Magna Carta*

You can see John's tomb in Worcester Cathedral. When it was opened in the eighteenth century, the King's skeleton was measured. Lackland was found to be just 5ft 5ins tall. Two of the surviving copies of Magna Carta from June 1215 can be seen at the British Library, with the other two at Lincoln and Salisbury Cathedrals.

Breay, Claire, *Magna Carta: Manuscripts and Myths* (London, The British Library), 2002.

AD 1225: *Hobbehod, Prince of Thieves*

Errol Flynn and Kevin Costner convey the fanciful modern vision. Holt, Keen and Spraggs explain how that vision developed over the centuries, with some fruitful comparisons to the legends of Hereward the Wake and highwaymen like Dick Turpin.

Holt, J. C., *Robin Hood* (London, Thames & Hudson), 1989.

Keen, Maurice *The Outlaws of Medieval Legend* (London, Routledge), 1987.

Spraggs, Gillian, *Outlaws and Highwaymen: The Cult of the Robber in England from the Middle Ages to the Nineteenth Century* (London, Pimlico), 2001.

AD 1265: *Simon de Montfort and his Talking-place*

A monument near Evesham Abbey beside the River Avon in Worcestershire recalls the death of Simon de Montfort on 4 August 1265, surrounded by the royalist forces and fighting against impossible odds. As a song of the time put it, it was 'the murder of Evesham, for *bataile non it was*'. Modern historians are sniffy about the work of Treharne, but he remains de Montfort's true historical disciple. Maddicott is more detached, and readable too.

Maddicott, J. R., *Simon de Montfort* (Cambridge, Cambridge University Press), 1994.
Treharne, R. F., *Simon de Montfort and Baronial Reform: Thirteenth-Century Essays*, ed. E. B. Fryde (London, Hambledon Press), 1986.

AD 1284: *A Prince Who Speaks No Word of English*

Jan Morris has composed the definitive Welsh diatribe demolishing the legend of the Prince of Wales. Caernarfon Castle itself, like Harlech, Conway and Edward's other great castles, survives triumphantly – as the eighteenth-century Welsh antiquarian Thomas Pennant put it, 'the magnificent badge of our servitude'. For full details consult the Welsh Historic Monuments website – www.cadw.wales.gov.uk. Professor Prestwich's survey of the Edwards is magisterial.

Morris, Jan, *The Princeship of Wales* (Llandysul, Gomer Press), 1995.
Prestwich, Michael, *The Three Edwards: War and State in England 1272–1377* (London, Weidenfeld & Nicolson), 1980.

AD 1308: *Piers Gaveston and Edward II*

Pierre Chaplais has recently advanced the argument that the relationship between Edward II and Piers Gaveston was non-sexual.

Nice try. Kenilworth Castle, home of 'the black hound of Arden', is well worth the visit. Originally fortified by King John, it later passed to John of Gaunt. Berkeley Castle is now a flash hotel, but the dungeon where Edward II met his agonising end is open to the public.

Chaplais, Pierre, *Piers Gaveston: Edward II's Adoptive Brother* (Oxford, Clarendon Press), 1994.

AD 1346: *A Prince Wins His Spurs*

At Nottingham Castle you can see the secret passage by which the young Edward III claimed his right to rule England. It is known as Mortimer's Hole, and is the only surviving part of the original twelfth-century motte-and-bailey fortress. For visiting times see www.nottinghamcity.gov.uk. Donald Featherstone's book is a fascinating study of the men and the weapon that got England off to such a deceptively good start in the Hundred Years War. Michael Packe died before he could finish his rich and idiosyncratic biography of Edward III, but it was well completed by L. C. B. Seaman.

Featherstone, Donald, *The Bowmen of England: The Story of the English Longbow* (Barnsley, Pen & Sword Books), 2003.
Packe, Michael, *King Edward III*, ed. L. C. B. Seaman (London, Routledge & Kegan Paul), 1983.

AD 1347: *The Burghers of Calais*

Auguste Rodin's melodramatic bronze makes up the curious quintet of historical monuments around the Houses of Parliament in Westminster. To the north, Boadicea, galloping beside the Thames in her scythe-wheeled chariot. To the west, Oliver Cromwell, looking stern. In the car park, Richard the Lionheart, with his sword raised towards Palestine. And to the south, in the public gardens, not far from the suffragette Emmeline Pankhurst, the six haggard burghers, dressed in rags and with ropes around their necks – six self-important Frenchmen decisively put in their place. The French clearly have a different view: the town of Calais commissioned Rodin to create the group of life-sized burghers in 1885, and the original casting stands outside the town hall – an enduring reminder of French fortitude in the face of English beastliness.

Sumption, Jonathan, *The Hundred Years War: Trial by Battle* (London, Faber), 1990.

AD 1347–9: *The Fair Maid of Kent and the Order of the Garter*

Every June the Queen processes through Windsor Castle with her modern fraternity of knights – who are not so Arthurian these days, counting politicians among their numbers and even a supermarket magnate, Lord Sainsbury of Preston Candover. At any time of year you can view the splendours of St George's Chapel and the rest of Windsor Castle, which started as a wooden motte-and-bailey structure. After centuries of embellishment, it is the finest actively functioning royal complex in the world: www.royal.gov.uk.

Collins, Hugh, *The Order of the Garter: Chivalry and Politics in Late Medieval England* (Oxford, Oxford University Press), 2000.

AD 1348–9: *The Great Mortality*

Philip Ziegler has written the definitive study of the Black Death with his usual erudition and grace. Norman Cantor's more recent study concentrates on the consequences. Rosemary Horrox offers a fine array of contemporary sources – not least the complaints that the plague reflected God's anger at indecent clothes and the disobedience of the young.

Cantor, Norman F., *In the Wake of the Plague: The Black Death and the World It Made* (London, Pocket Books), 2002.

Horrox, Rosemary (ed.), *The Black Death* (Manchester, Manchester University Press), 1994.

Ziegler, Philip, *The Black Death* (London, The Folio Society), 1997.

AD 1376: *The Bedside Manner of a Plague Doctor*

You can see examples of John Arderne's medical drawings for the removal of *fistulae in ano* and the gruesome surgical instruments he employed in Peter Murray Jones's well illustrated book.

Murray Jones, Peter, *Medieval Medicine in Illuminated Manuscripts* (London, The British Library), 1998.

AD 1377: *The Dream of Piers the Ploughman*

Set aside a day to read this rambling epic right through from beginning to end – preferably on a summer's afternoon, on a bank beside a stream in the Malvern Hills.

Langland, William, *Piers the Ploughman*, trans. and intro. J. F. Goodridge (London, Penguin Books), 1966.

AD 1381: *The 'Mad Multitude'*

Walk around the echoing arcades of modern Smithfield, and you can imagine under your feet the open meadow where Wat Tyler rode out on his pony to meet Richard II. If you get there early enough in the morning you can observe the porters and butchers of the modern meat-market, which will also, presumably, become part of history one day. Alastair Dunn's recent account of the Peasants' Revolt covers the ground of Melvyn Bragg's Radio 4 series. Dobson's classic volume presents readable extracts from all the main contemporary sources.

Dobson, R. B., *The Peasants' Revolt of 1381* (London, Macmillan), 1983.

Dunn, Alastair, *The Great Rising of 1381: The Peasants' Revolt and England's Failed Revolution* (Stroud, Tempus), 2002.

EXPLORING THE
ORIGINAL SOURCES

I hope this book leaves you with a curiosity – perhaps even a passion – for the original and earliest written sources on which our history is based. Julius Caesar relating his first sight of the white cliffs, Bede and his sparrow, Orderic Vitalis describing the survivors of the *White Ship* clinging to the wreckage in the night sea – these centuries-old writings need not be intimidating. To convey their flavour, I have tried to quote from the chronicles at some length, and I have also listed in the source notes the many lucid and accessible modern translations available, often in paperback.

But in recent years we have gained a still more accessible resource. Most of the great historical and classical texts are now available, free and on-line, via university websites. On www.georgetown.edu/faculty/ballc/oe/oe-texts.html, for example, you can find an index of sites that host electronic editions of Old English texts, translations and images of Anglo-Saxon manuscripts. By clicking on the listed links you can then access complete texts of works such as Bede's *Ecclesiastical History*, *Piers the Ploughman* and various versions of *Beowulf* – your own desktop digital scriptorium.

Three of these sites are particularly helpful. The Online Medieval and Classical Library at the University of California at Berkeley wwwsunsite.berkeley.edu/OMACL includes the complete text of the *Anglo-Saxon Chronicle*. At Fordham University, the Internet History Sourcebooks project, www.fordham.edu/halsall, covers ancient, medieval and modern history, arranging all the texts by topic. By looking under, say, 'slavery', or 'Roman sport and games', you can find a selection of texts on each subject. When you know what you are looking for, MIT's Classics website at http://classics.mit.edu is extremely fast, with over four hundred texts, mainly Graeco-Roman works, all in English translation and very clearly set out.

The on-line ventures of British universities cannot compare with the generously financed facilities of the US. But Reading University hosts a simply laid out, beginner-friendly site on www.library.rdg.ac.uk/subjects/ir/irclas.html, and the Institute of Historical Research at London University has an interesting, subject-based, on-line resources index which you can consult on www.history.ac.uk/ihr/resources/index.html.

Lege Feliciter, as the Venerable Bede would say – May you read happily!

ACKNOWLEDGEMENTS

History has been compared by the polymath Felipe Fernández-Armesto to 'a nymph glimpsed between leaves: the more you shift perspective, the more is revealed. If you want to see her whole you have to dodge and slip between many different viewpoints.' Peering through those leaves has been a consuming passion of my life, and my first thanks must be to the generations of historians and archaeologists whose research and analysis have parted so many branches. In the preceding source notes I set out the books on which I have relied, but I owe a particular debt to the historians on whose personal expertise and kindness I have drawn – Richard Eales, Dr David Hill, John McSween, Dr Simon Thurley, Professor Lynne Vallone and Yvonne Ward. Warm thanks to Patrick Wormald for the lunch and tea seminars at the Randolph, and to Professor Alfred Smyth for his unfailing elf-wisdom. Thanks to Elizabeth Finn in the archives at Canterbury and to Margaret Sparks, the cathedral historian; also to Dr Tony Trowles in the Muniments Room at Westminster Abbey. Nigel Rees helped me track down some elusive quotations through his newsletter. Philip Revill has dug out and explained the details of the National Curriculum. Thanks, as ever, to the partners of the John Sandoe bookshop and to the librarians and archivists at the London Library, the Public Record Office, and at my own, local, public library in the west minster.

There is a sense in which Peter Furtado, the editor of *History Today*, initiated this project by inviting me to contribute to his column on historical beginnings, 'Point of Departure'. It made me realise there was nothing I would enjoy more than re-examining the stories on which I was brought up – and it has reminded me of the debt I owe to the history teachers who encouraged me at Bristol Grammar School: Charles Peter Hill, Maurice Isaac, John Millward and Roy Avery. There were others, I might add, whose teaching and seminars my love of history survived.

I have written this book for adults – or, perhaps, for children of my own age – and I am grateful for the constructive criticism of certain younger readers: Rhian Carr, Jack George and, most of all, my younger son Bruno, who emailed me unsparing criticism while on his gap year in the Himalayas. This book is dedicated, however, to his elder brother Sasha – my wise, quiet and solid one. With three children I love and admire, and three volumes to offer in return for all the pride and delight they have given me, we shall proceed in order of seniority.

It has been a pleasure to write this book on my daily excursions to the kitchen table of Moyra Ashford who has researched, typed, checked and tried her best to keep me down to earth. As with other books, Jacqueline Williams has come to my rescue with the organising of the bibliography and many other areas of research. At Time Warner, my publishing team headed by David Young and Ursula Mackenzie has once again coped with a ferocious deadline. My special thanks to Peter Cotton, Sue Phillpott, Viv Redman, Tim Whiting – and to Roger Cazalet, inspirer of the woad plant, the cud-chewing cow and the other illustrations so brilliantly realised by Fred van Deelen.

This is my last book launched by my agent of so many years, Michael Shaw, but how kind of him to groom such an able successor in Jonathan Pegg. My greatest debt, as ever, is to my wife Sandi, support and critic, truest friend. If you like the little rose on the jacket – that was one of her ideas.

Robert Lacey, June 2003

INDEX